"For times of emergency the greatest gift you can give your loved ones is peace of mind. *The Loved Ones Kit* is peace of mind in a kit. It is the ultimate gift of information and intelligent planning. My family has a LOK, and so should yours."

~ *Robert G. Allen, best-selling author of* Multiple Streams of Income *and* Nothing Down; *co-author of* The One Minute Millionaire *and* Cracking the Millionaire Code

"*The Loved Ones Kit* is a no-nonsense guide filled with advice about addressing real-life concerns of death and dying. It shows you how to take care of practical matters in advance so your survivors have the freedom to grieve."

~ *Russell Friedman, co-author of* The Grief Recovery Handbook, When Children Grieve, *and* Moving On.

"Regardless of the systems and detailed contingency plans in the business world, we often fail to create the same in our personal lives. Jennifer Wilkov's LOK offers the perfect contingency plan for family, relatives and friends when dealing with the passing of a loved one. I've seen her put the kit into action, and have witnessed its benefits. No one should be without a LOK."

~ *Michael Love, President/CEO Steelcase Design Partnership*

"We live in a complex world in which handling personal emergencies doesn't have to be a nightmare. Jennifer Wilkov's LOK makes it simple and fun to find out the facts you need to cope, even in the worst situations."

~ *Rick Frishman, President, Planned TV Arts, and best selling coauthor of* Guerilla Publicity, Networking Magic *and* Author 101 *series*

The Loved Ones Kit

The enlightened way to organize your money and life for the ones you love

Jennifer S. Wilkov, CFP®

esp press

KNOW WHAT TO DO.™

Published by E.S.P. Press Corp.
A division of Evolutionary Strategic Planning, Inc.
189 Montague Street, Ste 900, Brooklyn, NY 11201, USA

The Loved Ones Kit by Jennifer S. Wilkov
Copyright © 2006 E.S.P. Press Corp.
All Rights Reserved

Design: YAY! Design
Illustrations: Julia Durgee

Printed in Mexico by R.R. Donnelley

ISBN 0-9777347-2-2

Additional copies of this book maybe purchased at a discount for educational, business, or sales promotional use by contacting the publisher through info@TheLOK.com.

Visit www.TheLOK.com and www.GetMyESP.com.

F or my beautiful grandmother Fay Wilkov:

The glorious life you led inspires me daily. Thank you for your shining example of community building. Your organizational talent, strength, leadership, tenacity, and communication skills have shown me how to be a member of a family, a team, and society. I am forever grateful for your generosity of spirit and your ability to make order out of chaos.

For my loved ones, Dad, Mom, and Jeffrey:

As my family and Core Team, you are phenomenal. Thank you for being there every step of the way.

I love you all very much.

E xpressing thoughts and ideas and traversing the highs and lows of book production so readers can ultimately learn and enjoy gives me a unique thrill. Each book project follows its own course, and the process of putting a book together involves the dedication of many people.

The gratitude I feel for the divine guidance I have received while working on this project runs deep. I'm grateful for the experience of working with so many talented individuals who have contributed their time, energy, effort, and insight to the book.

I especially honor the following people for their loving support and their faith in me:

My grandparents Abraham "Al" Wilkov and Fay Wilkov, for sharing their lives and humanity openly and elegantly with me and my family. Although they have both passed on (my grandmother died just before the book was completed), they live on inside my heart and soul. The videos our family has of them are priceless, and I'm grateful for the legacy of love they leave behind.

My grandparents Philip and Charlotte Hillsberg, for their generosity of spirit, their willingness to share their love and lives with us, and their shining example of self-expression. My grandfather passed away in the late '80s, but my grandmother Charlotte remains a beacon of bright light and an amazing presence in my life. I love her very much.

My Core Team is made up of my wonderful family: Marjorie and Howard Wilkov (Mom and Dad); my brother, Jeffrey, his beautiful wife, Kristina, and their children, Sydney Rachel and Logan Porter. Thank you for your loving support.

My clients, past and present, are an inspiration for me. I feel honored and blessed by their courage to speak up, to ask for assistance, and to pursue a relationship with money while living fully every day. I am grateful for the life experiences they have shared with me and for the opportunity to guide and assist them in their journey. Thank you for your ongoing trust and confidence.

I feel incredibly blessed because I have tremendous mentors and friends who enrich my life. They give 100 percent and are always there with kind words of encouragement and a warm hug. I want to thank my mentors and friends in the worlds of personal development, academia and formal education, and the martial arts Shintaido and Aikido. I hold admiration and respect for the individuals and mentors with whom I have literally and figuratively crossed paths: Anthony Robbins; Mark Victor Hansen; Robert G. Allen; T. Harv Eker; Joel and Heidi Roberts; Lauren Solomon; Blair Singer; Keith Cunningham; Dave Lakhani; Alex Mandossian; David Hancock; Albert Einstein; R. Buckminster Fuller; Walt Disney; H. F. Ito, Sensei; Don Cardoza, Sensei; Toshimitsu Ishii, Sensei; and others. Thank you for inspiring me.

I want to applaud the outstanding people in my company, Evolutionary Strategic Planning (ESP), specifically, Eileen Bonilla and Schonda Fields. These two talented women have understood the importance of the book. They have helped me in so many ways that I cannot find adequate words of gratitude. Thank you for your faith and contribution in this magical journey.

My championship team comprises many individuals who want more for me than I have ever imagined for myself. I want to recognize the contributions of David Halperin of Halperin & Halperin P.C., and the intellectual property team of Ross Charap, Myka Todman, and Elizabeth Corradino of Moses & Singer LLP, who have participated in every facet of the legal process imaginable to make this book a success. Steven Frushtick of Wiener Frushtick & Straub P.C. continues to be a phenomenal guide to IRS dos and don'ts. I thank you all for your deep commitment.

I especially want to thank the virtual publishing team that has made the book possible from conception, editorial, design, and illustration through to production, distribution, and publicity. The team's willingness to contribute talent, expertise, energy, and effort was a blessing for me. These people love books: Hats off to Liz Walker of Walker Publishing Services Inc., who brought together a phenomenal group of people. I salute her tenacity in getting the project produced gracefully. Editorial director Roberta Fineberg of A Muse Productions has once again opened her heart and mind and shared a unique talent for taking rough ideas and concepts and flowing them effortlessly into a final manuscript for readers to enjoy. Parlan McGaw of Golden Arts & Letters Inc. graciously copyedited and remained a tremendous support to the editorial process. Claire Wyckoff who initially stepped in to organize editorial content soon became both production editor and proofreader. Her ability to jump into the eclectic editorial mix and work diligently added tremendously to the success of the project. Billy Kelly of YAY! Design worked brilliantly as creative director and designer. I have enjoyed his flexibility, dedication, insight, and energetic creativity. Julia Durgee, illustrator, committed pen and ink to paper to create exceptional graphic novel illustrations that enliven the book. Her vivid comic book interpretations of the text are an inspiration.

For the audio version of the book, Barry Carollo of ADC Studios offered top-notch production experience to create a phenomenal CD. Barry is a talented audio engineer and producer in addition to being an extraordinary recording partner. From the bottom of my heart I thank you, your wife Susan, and son Joey for opening your hearts and home to me.

Kudos to Eric Kampmann and the fantastic team at Midpoint Trade Books for offering outstanding distribution support and sound advice to E.S.P. Press Corp. I especially want to applaud Gail Kump, Julie Hardison, and John Teall for their enthusiasm and guidance.

Rick Frishman of Planned TV Arts (PTA) is likewise extraordinary. Thank you for your insight, inspiration, and kindness. I'm also delighted to be working with Paul Schwartz as well as the whole team at PTA.

Lastly, I want to take a moment to acknowledge the reader. I admire and give a standing ovation for your courage and confidence to seek out guidance and information to reach your goals, desires, and dreams. I am honored to be an enthusiastic participant in your life.

Every book is a miracle of energy, creativity, thought, talent, collaboration, and support. Thank you, everybody, for the opportunity to share miracles.

Dating Your Money:
How to Build a Long-Lasting Relationship with Your Money in 8 Easy Steps

The Loved Ones Kit:
The Enlightened Way to Organize Your Money
and Life for the Ones You Love

A s I began writing *The Loved Ones Kit*, my beloved grandmother fell ill. While wrestling with the problem of our family member's deteriorating health condition, one of my relatives asked me to assist him with organizing her documents and information. He said to me, "We don't know what to do. We know where the documents are, but grandmother was always very private and did everything for herself. Where should we begin?"

It is truly no coincidence that my grandmother is passing at the same time the book is being written. Her passing is an incredible gift, and I must share with you, dear readers, what I have learned from my experience. I have seen the book in action -- what it creates, what it provides, the end result and blessings it bestows on a family in need.

My father, aunt and uncle all have expressed how much they appreciate what I have done to assist them. I feel it was my paternal grandmother's wish for me to complete the book in great haste since there are so many families like mine who need practical information to support their nearest and dearest for many years to come.

I completed *The Loved Ones Kit* in ninety days so I could get this user-friendly kit into your hands for the sake of your loved ones and yourself. I am passionate about the necessity of creating the kit because I have witnessed the anguish and frustration that family and friends experience when a calamity befalls someone they love and they don't have the basic practical information and documentation they need. I have watched people endure this situation as a result of not knowing how to—or not recognizing the need to—empower themselves and others with information.

The Loved Ones Kit (LOK)—Is it for you?

If you believe that having a will, a healthcare proxy and living will, power of attorney, and a fancy financial plan with charts and graphs and recommendations are what you need for your financial well-being and security…well, you may want to rethink your strategies.

As a Certified Financial Planner™ in large firms and subsequently a financial *pioneer* in my own business, I have lived through a myriad of life events with my clients. I have engaged in countless conversations about identify theft, infirm and dying parents, depressed spouses in long-term mental health institutions, seriously injured children, suddenly incapacitated friends who have no next of kin, alcoholic and/or drug-addicted relatives who need clinical care, etc. Admittedly it is difficult to be prepared for real-life emergencies, much less to give thought to locating paperwork, which suddenly becomes important at these times. In the cases of many of my clients, they were ready and able to assist but had no idea where the pertinent documents were. Since they didn't know where to find health records and names of doctors and were unable to access the person's accounts to cover the costs of unfortunate events, obtaining care for their family members and friends became a challenge. Knowing whom to notify in an emergency can be a mystery as an individual's information about employer contacts, organizations, and obligations may be unknown or not easily accessible.

For example, one of my clients had his computer stolen with all his personal information stored in his hard drive. He feared what thieves would do with his financial, banking, and credit card information. He was filled with anxiety when he thought about the real possibilities of a stranger exploiting this information. When I asked him for records of his important documents, account numbers, and contact information for financial professionals, he replied that he didn't have centralized records or files with that information. He would have to check his electronic organizers, peruse address books, thumb through Rolodexes, locate statements to verify his account numbers, and make numerous phone calls to get information.

In supporting another client during the death of her aunt to whom she was very close, I lived through the various phases of illness and death. My client came to me very distraught, came to terms with her emotions, and then focused on the practical issues of how to handle her beloved aunt's estate. No records or information were within easy reach—and as executor of the will, she was left to put together the financial pieces of her aunt's life. Since there were no immediate family members to assist her, it took some time to settle the matter.

A third client had a close friend who died in the London Subway bombing in 2005— a terrible tragedy that rocked the world and made everybody question mortality and international safety. The friend who passed was thirty-eight years old and had never thought about making financial arrangements in the event of an unforeseen circumstance. The young man's family and friends' pain and agony were unbearable as

Can one prepare emotionally, spiritually, and sensibly for unavoidable situations?

was the weight of their unanswered questions of "why him, why now?" Listening to my client, who was the best friend of the young man who died, I wondered: Can one prepare emotionally, spiritually, and sensibly for unavoidable situations?

While organized documentation and clear financial plans will not assuage the feelings family and friends have when they rush in to assist a person in crisis, having such information at hand can eliminate a lot of the stress and tension they would otherwise experience. What if a person could create his or her own instructional kit in which loved ones could find information easily about the owner's finances, health-care providers, medical and mental health history, prescriptions and health-care supplements, business associates, financial contacts, attorney, accountant, community involvement, and charitable interests before a catastrophe hit? In a crisis situation anybody could jump in and locate whatever pertinent information was considered vital to assist the person in need. In other words, having medical information in a kit could save a life. In addition, it is a comfort to kith and kin to have access to financial documentation so that finances remain intact as the healing process runs its natural cycle. When the patient returns to her regular daily life, she is not faced with unpaid bills, late fees, mounting debts, collection notices, utility disconnections, etc. In the unfortunate event of death, loved ones have all the financial information required to expedite the estate settlement process effectively and can fend off any false claims made against the estate of the deceased.

Creating Your LOK

Does mapping out practical information—such as creating lists of personal health and financial information so that loved ones know how to help you in case you become sick or injured—sound like your style of communication? In putting together instructions for loved ones, you may feel self-conscious, anxious, superstitious about death, benevolent, noble—or none of the above. Before embarking on a journey to organize your money and life to help others help you in case of a crisis, you need to explore your feelings on lofty subjects such as your own mortality and karma. If you were ever in a serious accident, who would take care of you? Not the most comforting of questions, granted, but—whatever your answers are—here is where you can start:

1. *Behind the Loved Ones Kit (LOK). Live life with passion knowing that if you need some assistance, you have a LOK™ and in it is all the information anybody could ever need to be effective and helpful in an emergency. A LOK™ fills both a spiritual and practical need for putting together vital information before something unexpected occurs. Build the kit for the ones you love—and they'll love you forever. Call it good karma.*

2. *Prepare It. Let's face it—it's time to gather your material and work on your LOK™. Think about and name situations where a Loved Ones Kit™ would be the first item someone reaches for in an emergency. Either you'll get lucky because your loved ones have telepathic powers, or you'll give them keys to your LOK™ so they'll know where to go for help.*

3. *Crack the LOK Code. What, where, and how to access it? Don't rely on your family and friends' extrasensory perception. If it's prepared properly, your loved ones will be able to put their hands on the information they need for whatever calamity arises. Either you do your research today on your finances and the myriad of vital statistics for the kit, or your loved ones will be forced to brave it alone tomorrow. Get it together efficiently and effectively.*

4. *LOK In Your Documents. Research the materials you need to include in the kit, and organize all your pertinent data in neat categories. You may want to work online, systematizing the data electronically and then arranging all your hard copy agreements in one central location. Focus on getting the job done in whatever fashion resonates with your style.*

5. *Key to Your Connections. Who are the people who assist you with your health and wealth? Make a list and check it. Include health providers and financial professionals in your LOK™ so that your loved ones will know who to contact on your behalf. Share information with the people you love.*

6. *Un-LOK Your Life. Think of the LOK™ as a record or diary of your input and participation in the world. The kit provides insight into your day-to-day contributions to society, including the organizations you belong to and activities you participate in. Empower your loved ones with the kit—an outpouring of love intended for communication with those whom you cherish most in your life. They'll be relieved to find the information treasure trove you've stored away for them*

7. *Use It. A LOK™ is not a doorstop, coaster, or welcome mat. Dismiss any plans of hiding the kit on the top row of the bookshelf. The LOK™ is created not to gather dust but to be a handy reference used to check in with your constantly evolving self. Celebrate your efforts in putting this vital information together and learn how to use the kit effectively for you and your loved ones.*

8. *Update It. Recognize life events that trigger changes, which means you have to update your LOK™. Learn to check information annually to keep your LOK™ fresh and accurate.*

"Namaste" (very special acknowledgments)

Providing pertinent information for emergency situations, *The Loved Ones Kit* is a user-friendly tool for you and your loved ones. An enlightened approach to taking care of yourself and caring for others in a modern world, it is your spiritual and practical guide—leading you and others to greater knowledge of your comings and goings in the universe. Your LOK™ mantra: Vital information about myself is accessible and easy to find for my own use and for my loved ones.

Finally, if you are wrestling with the idea that you don't need a kit "'cause I'm covered," put yourself in the shoes of those you love and ask yourself the following question: "Do I want my loved ones to have to go searching for my medical and financial information in the event that I'm not around to show them where it is? Do I really want them to have to search high and low for my vital information in order to assist me or fulfill my wishes for my health and wealth?"

When you think about how useful the kit is, you may end up purchasing the book for everyone you know. Your loved ones will thank you for it—and one day you may thank them for their kit.

Eight words of practical wisdom: Live fully, passionately, and beginning today, live confidently.

Phase

1

Behind the
Loved Ones Kit (LOK)

*Learn
compassion…*

Working as an information expert over the years, I have learned that the best way to organize your vital data is to keep it in one easy-to-find place. Centralizing your personal information provides you with an immediate record of all your financial dealings. Should there be any threats of identity theft or if your credit cards are lost or stolen, you know where to look for information to handle whatever situation arises. In short, a LOK™ is a graceful and elegant way of collecting your information so that your relationship to finances remains clear during stressful times.

The LOK™ comes in all shapes and sizes, and is created by you for the end user. The information can be collected in a binder, folio, or series of folders in a filing cabinet. If you are electronically inclined, your data can be stored in files on your computer in which you can save information and scanned copies of important documents. Whether electronic or hard copy, a collection of simple facts (your financial records, legal documents, health history, contact numbers and addresses, among other important pieces of information) is stored in file folders for someone else to have access in case of an emergency.

Lucky to Have a LOK

In my practice over the years, I have met with countless families and facilitated difficult discussions about planning for misfortune. Unexpected tragedies happen to all of us: They are challenges, and *The Loved Ones Kit* helps us to be prepared for the many tests in our lives. If you are not able to help yourself, who do you expect will step in when random bad luck sets you back? Let me point out that the flip side of an unfortunate circumstance is a propitious opportunity—and I am delighted to say that the clients who have successfully embraced planning for disaster are the same people who live fully each and every day.

The focus of a lot of family meetings these days is often an aging parent. Many of my clients have to deal with infirm mothers and fathers, and I have talked with them about how to navigate the medical maze and wind through the family finances. I have also learned that regardless of age, everyone benefits from gathering and organizing critical personal information for the sake of loved ones. This is especially true for family members who live alone—not only the elderly but also young urban men or women far from home. Does this sound like your situation?

Learning to sustain our cherished family members, relatives, and friends in a community connected increasingly by virtual reality and technology, we need to be briefed about our loved ones and keep them in the loop. Sharing information with one another is critical to our well-being and survival especially when we need assistance. The need for simple and clear instructions becomes essential during an emergency in a post-modern era in which many people are increasingly independent.

In eight phases, I show you how to create your own Loved Ones Kit™. You learn how to navigate challenging times, ultimately making life joyful because you know you are covered in an awkward situation. My goal is to address that voice I've been hearing throughout the years about people's needs to communicate their vital information more fully in cases of accidents, emergencies, illnesses, or other unforeseen circumstances for those whom they love. Think of a LOK™ as a spiritual insurance policy, in which your loved ones find a treasure trove of information about you that helps them know how to assist you quickly, effectively, and lovingly.

Unspoken Requests

The Loved Ones Kit is designed for you—and somebody who does not have a set of instructions to assist you should something unexpected happen. Because the number eight represents unlimited fortune in both Japanese culture and in Feng Shui (the Chinese art of placement) *The Loved Ones Kit* has been divided into eight phases. Each phase is designed to guide you gently through information you want to collect, how to organize it, and how to make the information in the kit accessible so your loved ones can best assist you. You'll also have all the tools to develop a kit for a loved one, for example, a parent whose information you want to have on hand during an emergency.

Complete the activities associated with each phase as if you were an explorer looking for buried treasure. At the end of the process, you will have created the ultimate treasure chest for you and your loved ones that will save everyone pain, frustration, and heartache because they will find information fast when it is needed most.

Count on Your LOK

As we grow and evolve, there are key moments in our lives when we need quick access to our ever-changing financial and health information. Yet, some of us still think that gathering data is not particularly useful or urgent. As a result we delay, procrastinate, or downplay the importance of storing and updating pertinent personal information.

During times of difficulty, your loved ones can count on the LOK™ that you have painstakingly assembled. Your relationship to your LOK™ begins here. Fortune-tellers may be able to predict your fate with a modicum of accuracy, but a LOK™ is a true expression of your free will: An insightful and spiritual approach to collecting data, the LOK™ has been designed to prepare for the unforeseeable.

"I'm gonna live forever…"

Most of us at every age think that we are going to live forever. It's a very human feeling. We feel invincible, that nothing will ever affect, afflict, or harm us. The normal reaction to tragedy is to deny it, push it away, or comfort ourselves with the thought: "That would never happen to me."

Think you're immortal? Do you feel unconsciously that you're beyond the human realm—that you're invincible? Join the club. The culture feeds into your desire to want to live forever. In contemporary society, age 50 is the new 30. Everybody wants to remain young. Why? People put off growing older by exercising, eating healthy foods, and cosmetic surgery. So where's the natural lifecycle in all of this? Does this mean that you will remain healthy forever?

"The unexamined life is not worth living"
—Socrates

Does it mean you will never suffer a disaster or know someone who has a life-threatening disease? You will never, ever, under any circumstances, expire…right?

Ask yourself this: As an all-powerful being, are you comfortable with your safety net? If you feel vulnerable because you don't have one or don't know how to create greater security in your life, you may not be living fully because you may be stuck in a fear of the unforeseen. The fifth-century B.C. Greek philosopher Socrates said: "The unexamined life is not worth living." Although he said this because he loved philosophy and was defending his role as a philosopher in ancient Greece, his assertion has practical application today. If you are not willing to look at your life squarely and honestly, you are living in a shadow of existence in which your anxieties are getting the best of you. Denial is a manifestation of fear—so if Plan A ("I'm gonna live forever") doesn't work out you may want to consider a Plan B. If you are concerned about your safety and welfare in the world and at the same want to live freely and passionately, you've got to get a LOK™.

We make choices every day about how we live. In some areas of our lives, we are wild and crazy, push the limits of our physical strength, and challenge our abilities. In other realms we go easy on ourselves, retreat, settle down because of desire, expectations, concerns, fears, or unexpected health conditions.

In the popular song "Live Like You Were Dying," by Tim McGraw, a man changes his life after being diagnosed with an illness. The song is about a man who chooses to live more fully (skydiving, mountain climbing, and bull riding as new ways of experiencing life) and deeply (becoming a caring father, involved husband, and committed friend).

When you think about your life, are you someone who likes pushing the envelope? Do you participate fully in the lives of others, enjoying family, friends, and mates? Are you cautious when making choices on how to live your daily life?

Are you filled with anxiety about keeping your world germ-free, staying away from polluted areas, or not taking on physical challenges that you feel will be dangerous?

When we haven't organized our personal information, we are taking risks with our health and wealth. Whether or not you have easy access your health and financial data affects your comfort level and your ability to be present in the moment. You may go skydiving or climb the highest mountain peak, and, I guarantee, you'd engage differently in these activities (among others) if you knew your life was in order. Subconsciously, when our lives become disorganized, we experience anxiety, which creates blocks to personal growth.

In the unlikely event that something disastrous occurs—to you, the invincible and immortal one, or to a loved one—what is your Plan B, *just in case*?

Plan B—Just in Case

Think of the Loved Ones Kit™ as buried treasure. It's a strongbox of information about your vital statistics for you and the ones you love. It's not a financial plan, and it is not limited to legal documents, such as a will you may or may not have completed with your attorney.

The Loved Ones Kit™ is a compassionate, thoughtful approach for gathering vital information about your finances, health, and other pertinent details about your life. It centralizes personal data in an easy-to-understand format. You and loved ones can access it for information fast in the event that you are compromised in any way and need assistance. The LOK™ is a roadmap leading to you.

Spiritual Attitude

The Loved Ones Kit™ provides practical and spiritual protection for you and the ones you love. When something happens to a family member, the clan knows where to go for information. Instead of being at odds with one another over conflicting data, family members can instead rally around the sibling, parent, child, or grandparent who needs help. By centralizing everybody's information, you create a sense of protection for the entire family.

Getting comfortable with the inevitability of challenging situations and unexpected hardships in life, and in those of family and friends, you begin to understand that you can prepare for unfortunate experiences by building a LOK™. If you're superstitious, you may wonder about putting together this information at all. Is it an invitation to disaster and heartache? After reflecting on your reasons for compiling material for a LOK™, you will discover that helping others help you is an act of loving-kindness. Remember: the energy you put out into the universe comes back to you. The careful preparation of your Loved Ones Kit™ for family and friends will boomerang out into the universe and be returned one hundredfold. The spiritual take is: If you have positive thoughts and are well-intentioned towards others, your behavior comes back to you and is paid in kind. The LOK™ is an affirmative tool for *paying it forward*. It sets you free to explore the world.

Whether you provide information about your LOK™ with family and friends immediately after you have finished assembling it, or whether you choose to let them know in due time, you are in the process of paying

it forward and creating good karma in the community. The Loved Ones Kit™ is both an invitation and manual for building community. Everybody benefits when becoming a caretaker, and alternately by being cared for. It is one of the greatest gifts that a society can offer its members.

Without the stress, frustration, and pain of trying to figure out where information is hidden, anybody can jump in and be effective in a crisis. People can teach each other about building a LOK™, and the spiritual cycle of protection will span generations to come. Spread the LOK™.

True Love in a LOK

When something unfortunate occurs, you're covered, baby! Not to worry. You have taken the right steps to rally support and to assist those who facilitate your recovery. In building a LOK™, you exercise free will on the journey—you are solely responsible for generating all the valuable information that goes inside the kit. The data becomes your key to enjoying greater ease and security as you venture forth in the world. As a result of your positive actions, you have ensured a positive experience for everyone. Is this not the truest expression of love?

It's just your LOK™!

Phase

2

Prepare It

*Be loved
forever...*

Ready to put together a LOK™ for yourself or for your loved ones? Do you want an electronic kit (documents saved in file folders on your desktop) or a hard copy kit (a physical kit with all your vital information)? Maybe you want both an electronic kit (stored on a CD) and a physical kit—documents in a filing cabinet or expandable files, paperwork stored in a banker's box, sheets in a three-ring binder, loose papers stored in a strong box or safe deposit box, or materials stashed in a monogrammed leather briefcase?

Phase 2 answers your questions about where to start, what you need, how to pull it all together, and how long it takes. The phase also discusses where to store your documents and how to back it all up so your work is not lost.

Where to Start

There are different styles of kits, so let's examine the following types based on convenience, size, form, cost, and storage space.

Many people like a hard copy kit because it's portable—easy to pick up and go. It requires no computers, cords, or electricity to access material. A hard copy kit includes an index in a binder, folio, expandable files, file folders in a filing cabinet, or stylish briefcase or portfolio. You can spend anywhere from $10 to $250 to store your kit—from that simple binder to a filing cabinet or leather briefcase. Binders are easy to store on any shelf in a bedroom, kitchen, den, living room, or study. An expandable file is inexpensive, and is small enough to be placed on a closet shelf, under a bed, in a desk drawer or cabinet, or in a kitchen pantry. A filing cabinet or file drawers on wheels isn't cheap, but the office furniture may be convenient should you have a lot of paperwork and need extra storage space. Filing cabinets can be expensive, costing upwards of $100, and do require space. A stylish briefcase or portfolio, such as embossed leather or monogrammed canvas, may be an item you wish to spend some money on. Do any of these styles of kits resonate with your personal method of organizing information?

Maybe you prefer organizing your data on computers, where you consolidate information in an electronic format that is quick, inexpensive, and easy to access from anywhere. A digital LOK™ is mobile and is easily accessed from your computer, laptop, CD-ROM, or a portable hard drive, where information can be stored and backed up. An electronic LOK™ may appeal to you especially if you own a home computer or laptop, a scanner, and can back up material. You'll need to scan all your documents that are not already in electronic file form. If you receive online statements for bills, bank, and investment accounts, you can set up directories or files on your computer for this information so that you and others can find it fast. Search features on the computer make documents very easy to find in cases when files are moved mistakenly to another folder or directory.

Getting It Together

Beginning with Phase 2, there is a list of materials you'll need to gather to complete your LOK™. For subsequent phases, refer back to the list to help you put your kit together successfully.

The following are sources of information you'll need to access to build a kit: address books, Rolodexes, personal digital assistant (PDA) files, electronic contact information systems, legal documents, insurance policies, bank and investment statements, bills and invoices for recurring services you employ, pet information, your wallet, driver's license, social security information, credit cards, loan data, and legal documents, among other material. Start with the information listed above to gather your pertinent information for the kit.

Your information is divided into the five following categories.

1. **Personal Information:** *birth certificate; social security number; passport; permanent and summer addresses; names and addresses of family members; emergency contacts; name of employer; military records.*

2. **Medical Documentation:** *names of doctors and health practitioners; medical conditions; prescription medicines; natural or homeopathic medicines; vitamin supplements; allergies; blood type; medical history; medical insurance policies (including prescription, dental and vision information); Medicare and Medigap plan information; long-term care policy; health care proxy and living will.*

3. **Financial Data:** *bank accounts; investment accounts; tax returns; loan information; credit cards; real estate investment documents; fine art; life insurance policy; homeowners insurance policy; automobile insurance policy; umbrella insurance policy; deeds and mortgages; monthly bills; monthly income statements; appraisals; business investment and ownership obligations.*

4. **Legal Records:** *pre- or post-nuptial agreements; marriage license; adoption papers (children); guardianship; separation agreement; divorce decree; maintenance/child support agreements; business partnerships; power of attorney; will.*

5. **Community Activities:** *religious practice and affiliations; fundraising; charitable organizations; volunteering; professional and networking groups; health and fitness clubs and activities; social clubs; political activism.*

Packaging this information into a kit is very workable, especially when you've decided where to collect the data and how to store it. If you already have office furniture and/or an electronic filing system, start organizing your information into the categories above: *Personal Information; Medical Documentation; Financial Data; Legal Records; and Community Activities.*

Testing Your LOK

In building a LOK™, reflect on the following question: Do you access information in the same fashion that your loved ones do? Think about the amount of information you need to amass and about how you can make it all accessible to your loved ones in a flash. Don't feel intimidated by the voluminous material. Stay on target: Help your loved ones help you. Keep them in mind at all times as the end users. They are your special audience. Make the finished kit easy to use, and consider that your life may depend on others ability to access it.

For example, what if you are building a digital LOK™ for yourself, but your parents are not technologically inclined and don't use a computer? Hard copy backup would be essential in this case. If your parents aren't computer savvy, they may have a tough time accessing vital materials on your computer. Maintain the digital LOK™ as your style of communication, but just in case have hard copy on hand.

With both a digital and hard copy LOK™, your loved ones are an effective team in the event of a crisis. For example, a digital version of your LOK™ can be sent to your brother or sister in California, while your parents in New York refer to a hard copy version. Should you reside, say, in Washington, DC, and something unexpected befalls you, your parents in New York can rush to your side while your sibling in California makes all the necessary calls to medical professionals about your care.

> "The LOK™ is designed for you and someone else intervening on your behalf."

The LOK™ is designed for you and someone else intervening on your behalf. Make your kit easy to find. If you require assistance in an unfortunate circumstance, a loved one can locate the kit quickly and effortlessly. You will have someone you trust on the spot. A highly accessible kit translates into you getting greater support when you need it most.

Hiring a LOK Specialist

Are you ambivalent about putting together a LOK™? Seems time consuming? Do you feel it may be difficult to create a LOK™ by yourself? Working with a professional—someone trained to facilitate the process seamlessly and assuage your anxiety and frustration—may be the right move.

Should you opt to work with a specialist to complete your LOK™, I recommend someone who has been certified. Specialists are carefully trained, and their experience contributes greatly to the quality of the final version of your LOK™. The specialist can work with you in person or by phone. She or he will help you build your LOK™ in either a hard copy or electronic version, and you can create it in less time than you would imagine. The specialist keeps a copy of your LOK™ in a fireproof location. Keep her contact information in an accessible place so she can be reached during an emergency situation. Should you or your loved ones require assistance from the specialist, she will have a toll-free number where she can be reached and access your information within twenty-four hours. If you live on your own, you may want to hire a LOK Specialist™.

Backing Up Your LOK

At the outset of the LOK™ project, consider how you plan to back up your data. If you are working with hard copy documents, I suggest you create two copies of your LOK™. Keep one copy in your home and one copy in a location that is accessible to others. If you store your papers in a strongbox or lockbox that requires a key or combination, give someone access in the event your primary copy cannot be found. If you are using a digital LOK™, store your information on your computer and save a copy on a CD, DVD, memory stick, or separate hard drive. The copy should likewise be stored in a safe location. Back up your information in whatever form or style suits you and your loved ones best so that your LOK™ remains secure.

Chomping at the Bit

I know the most important question on your mind is, "How long will it take to build a LOK™?" For most people, the task appears daunting and they think it will take days, weeks, or even a lifetime to create a kit.

Surprisingly, the LOK™ can be completed in as little time as four hours if you are prepared. If you have all the documents you need, the LOK™ builds itself. The kit is created over several sessions, so don't rush to complete it. The key is making a commitment to get it together—methodically, conscientiously, and carefully—so you get it done to help yourself and those you love. The time you invest now to complete the kit will pay twofold when someone you love reaches for it. Coming to your aid, your loved ones will have no time to waste and will need all the information they can get their hands on.

> **"If you are prepared the LOK™ can be completed in a few short hours."**

Take a few minutes to reflect on your availability to create a LOK™. Can you squeeze in the time? My answer is: You can't afford not to! Protecting yourself and the ones you love is too important. Once committed to building a LOK™, you will feel empowered knowing that you are securing the future.

Let's finish what we started.

3

Crack the LOK Code

*Delight in
the details...*

L et's get down to it: Have handy all the information and documents that were mentioned in Phase 2 because Phase 3 is about extracting important data and organizing it into an instantly accessible, easy-reference summary of your vital information. Keeping in mind the five categories—*Personal Information, Medical Documentation, Financial Data, Legal Records, and Community Activities*—you will be sorting and sifting through these materials to find what you need.

Form and Substance

In Phase 2, you determined what kind of kit you would create—hard copy, electronic, or maybe both. As you gather papers and data necessary for building the LOK™, you may realize that the information you need is scattered all over the place. In order to arrange the information, you need to have a system so you can move quickly through the five categories. To assist you with organizing the data, first go to www.TheLOK.com. Download the LOK Details Worksheet™, which will guide you through your jumble of paperwork. If you are building a hard copy LOK™, print out the file. If you are working on an electronic LOK™, the worksheet files can be filled out online and stored directly in folders or directories on your desktop. Follow the guidelines and you will find the LOK™ actually builds itself. Organizing a LOK™ for yourself or for a loved one is an intuitive process once you get into the groove.

One of my clients, Sally, was building a kit for herself. She printed out the LOK Details Worksheet™. Having on hand the various materials and documents listed in Phase 2, she followed the Worksheet checklist and found that by organizing even a small portion of her data, she created an easy reference. When Sally needed documentation for overseas travel (passport number, U.S. driver's license for documentation to drive abroad, health insurance information), she had a reference guide. Because Sally had contact information at her fingertips, she could make inquiries fast. In the process, she discovered that her health insurance would not cover her outside the United States. For that trip she had to obtain a separate policy, which her health insurance agent brokered.

Details, Details, Details

Let's face it: The categories *Personal, Medical, Financial, Legal, and Community* take you by the hand to organize your LOK™. Let's take a look at *Personal Information*, since the LOK™ is all about you. Using the worksheet as a trusty guide, fill in these details: your full legal name and any other names you go by; date and place of birth; social security number; driver's license number and state of issuance; passport number; and health insurance company, including policy number, personal identification number (PIN), and contact numbers. If you have supplementary or third-party insurance such as Medicare, note this and include all plan names and contact information. As for your car, include your vehicle identification number (VIN), license plate number, and registration date. Lastly include your familial situation: spouse's name; dates and state location of marriage, separation, or divorce; and children's names and birth dates.

Are you still with me? The next section may demand a little more concentration and elbow grease to fill in the blanks for your "in case of emergency" contacts. This self-explanatory list includes contact information for your family and next of kin: immediate family (spouse, son, daughter, father, mother, siblings) and close relatives; friends of the family; your primary doctor(s); your healthcare proxy; the executor/executrix of your will; your estate attorney; elder law attorney; accountant; financial planner; and LOK Specialist™. Include all employer information. If you are in the military, include your rank, station of service, and a contact person you would like to be notified in an emergency situation. If you are in a union, include any and all contact information about it. Finally, are there any people not on your list whom you would like contacted in the event that something unexpected happens to you? Be sure to add their names and any pertinent instructions necessary, say, for taking care of a pet you own: e.g., the name and contact number of a dog walker, kennel, pet caretaker, and/or veterinarian in case your pet requires care in your absence.

The Doctor Is In

In the spaces provided in the *Medical Documentation* section of the LOK Details Worksheet™ record the contact information for your primary doctor, specialists, dentist, and other healthcare practitioners you see regularly. Women, please add the name and telephone number of your gynecologist.

Remember: Note any chronic health conditions for which you receive medical attention on a regular basis or for which you consult alternative health care practitioners. Be specific and keep your facts straight: Write down the name of each professional and the problem she treats.

Got allergies? Jot them down. If taking penicillin gives you a nasty rash, let your loved ones know about it. If you don't know what you are allergic to you may want to consider doing allergy testing. Consult your doctor. Also note your blood type. And if you don't know your blood type, find out. Ask your physician to provide this information from your medical file. You can also locate this information if you have ever donated blood. When you make a blood donation, your blood type is identified and often included on the donation card. Otherwise get a blood type test or ABO, which classifies blood into one of four types: A, B, AB, or O. The Rh blood type test checks for the presence (+) or absence (-) of the Rh antigen (also called the Rh factor). Place all this vital information diligently in your kit.

My client Jason was putting together his information in a kit when he realized that he didn't know his blood type. He contacted his primary physician. Jason got the information he needed and put it in his LOK™. The worksheet prompted him to take stock of the vitamins he was taking. No one, including his physician, had ever asked him for such specific information on the supplements he took. He was very grateful for the process since it provided him an opportunity to examine what he was doing to maintain his health.

Now, take a look at the supplements and vitamins you use to maintain your good health. List the health supplements you use, including all vitamins, herbs, and other natural products. Be specific about the daily dose. If you take two tablets of Pinellia, a health supplement, three times a day to treat lung congestion, note it. In addition make a list of the prescription drugs you take: Mark down the name of the medicine, dosage, and physician who prescribed it.

Last but not least, let's tackle health insurance. Dig out the following information from wherever you keep it: your health insurance card with group policy number, personal identification number, members' services contact information, and mailing address. If you have Medicare or a Medigap supplemental policy, your LOK™ should include specifics, i.e., the name, type of policy you possess, and the company providing coverage. Jot down in your *Medical Documentation* worksheet any additional policy numbers from these special plans. For long-term care policies, you need only to include the name of the insurance company, phone number, agent's name, policy number, daily benefit amount, and whether your policy includes home care coverage.

Show Me the Money

Do you have stacks of documents with important financial data piled into different drawers in your office or home? Is your money scattered about in commercial institutions or spread out into multiple accounts? We'll make a push *now* to organize all those random financial details into one location, the *Financial Data* section of your LOK™, where you can quickly and easily plug into your money data.

You will need to refer to your account statements, bankbooks, and checkbooks. Proceed to make a record of all the places where you have your money, include names of banks, branch locations, and bank contacts. Let's begin with your accounts, including checking, savings, and money market investments. Are you the sole account holder, or do you have joint accounts? In your kit, provide all names on all accounts, as well as account numbers, routing numbers, and the people with whom you have a financial connection at the various institutions.

Do the same for your investment accounts: include the name of the institution, office address, name(s) on the account, account number, particular person(s) with whom you have a financial relationship, and type of account (e.g., brokerage, IRA, private placement, etc.). Also add to the LOK Details Worksheet™ the month and year you began working with a given institution and your advisors.

Make a list of sources of income: Where does your money come from? How often do you receive income? How much do you receive? Is your income deposited directly into an account? Enter the facts and figures in your LOK™.

Moving on to loan and credit card information, fill in the worksheet with the names of institutions, name(s) on each account, type of account (mortgage, credit card, line of credit, etc.), account numbers, contact phone numbers, frequency of payment, minimum amount due, interest rate, and a list of the money folks with whom you deal regularly. Credit cards have additional numbers on the back to prove to banks that the plastic is really yours. Record the last three numbers, a.k.a. the three-digit code, from the back of each credit card (or the last four digit code found on the front of American Express cards), as well as the expiration date. Don't stop now! Include the month and year you began each account. Which accounts are for which bills? Please detail how the bills are paid: In case of an emergency your loved ones, with the expert guidance of your kit, will know which bills to pay immediately and from which accounts. Aha!

> "Relieve your loved ones from a world of confusion...."

Bills you pay routinely are also included in the *Financial Data* section. For a quick rundown of what you pay to whom, put this list in your kit: the names of each payee, billing cycle (monthly, quarterly, etc.), amounts due, mailing addresses for payments, and business contact people and phone numbers (employee names and telephone extension numbers). Remember: Indicate which account(s) you draw from to pay the bills.

Doing detective work on a loved one's finances is stressful. Figuring out which bills are to be paid through which accounts is a headache. Relieve your loved ones from a world of confusion by helping them crack your LOK™ code: Give them the material they need in the kit to do what they have to do to keep your finances on track.

Other information to consider for your *Financial Data* files: Are you a partner in a business? For businesses owned, list the address for each business, your percentage of ownership, contact information for the partners in the business, and your attorney and accountant for each business. If you have real estate, make a list of your properties: location of the real estate, ownership in each investment, names of any partners with whom you jointly own property, partner contact information, and contact numbers for both the attorney and accountant who work with you on real estate issues. If you're a collector of luxury goods, you'll want to provide names of reputable appraisal companies for your art, jewelry, automobiles, and other collectibles.

Having information about your insurance coverage will be crucial to your loved ones in any emergency situation. Remember to follow the worksheet, which is an excellent guide to list making. There are many types of insurance; in your LOK™ include information about the policies you possess. List the name of the company holding your policy, the type of policy, the policy number, the original date of the policy, the premium amounts, payment schedule, contact information, and insurance agent's name and phone number. Whose name is the policy in? Who are the policy beneficiaries? Get it all down! Do you have insurance policies through your employer? Note them—and include all the contact information for the human resource department at your company. Pension accounts, such as 401(k), 403(b), or annuities through your employer or union, should be listed too. This information should include the name of the company the account is connected to, account number, and a PIN number (if applicable).

Legal Beagle

What does it take to organize your *Legal Records*? You may find this category easier to manage than the previous ones. The only information you need for your legal file is the contact information for your attorneys and the location where you keep the original copies of your documents. The LOK™ is the best location to keep photocopies of all your important legal documents. In the event of an emergency, your loved ones can be in touch effortlessly with the legal team referred to in the kit.

It Takes a Village

We're almost there. The last element concerns *Community Activities*. If you are affiliated with a religious congregation, social or political organizations, list contact people and phone numbers in the event you have an accident, are seriously ill, in the hospital, or pass away. Imagine if one day you just stopped showing up at meetings and events and nobody knew your whereabouts. Your colleagues would be worried by your sudden absence. Provide contact information for each of the networks, organizations, and charity groups you are active with. Your loved ones will want the community to be in the know should something adverse happen to you. By including contact information, your loved ones can make quick phone calls to keep your relationship with those colleagues intact. Those friends and volunteers may even provide unexpected support.

Putting It All Together

If you have broken out in a sweat, I understand: The LOK™ requires getting together a lot of data. If you've had the courage to follow through on the worksheets, you will find all your information in one place. That's the payoff! The investment of time you are making will save hours and hours of frustration in the future for you and your loved ones. If locating and organizing your data has been time consuming for *you*, just imagine how much time it would take your loved ones to get it together. The Loved Ones Kit™ has the power to save your life during a medical emergency, to provide identification information in the event of an accident or identity theft, furnish insurance and medical information to a hospital, and transmit special instructions for your loved ones when you cannot communicate with them. Just think how confidently and fully you can enjoy life, knowing that all those pesky details people need to know in case of an emergency are now easy to find in your LOK™. No divining rod needed to find signposts of your life along the way— your loved ones have everything they need at a glance and in one place.

From my perspective, delight is in the details. The easier data can be found, the more delightful is the outcome.

4

LOK in Your Documents

*Create order
from chaos…*

Y ou are at your desk, contemplating the document sections of your LOK™. Surrounded by literally masses of materials, you size up the data. Each document has a purpose and is necessary for a given situation. How many different documents are you looking at? Can you imagine your loved ones putting their hands on these materials if you were unable to tell them where the documents could be found? Phase 4 is all about organizing your paperwork. With the help of a cohesive, intuitive system, your loved ones avoid playing "hide and seek" with important information.

Getting Your Papers in Order

When working with a myriad of documents, you will want a clean surface and lots of space to sift through, sort out, and arrange your material. A dining room table, desk, or conference room table in an office is perfect for the job. As you filter through papers, ID cards, and photocopies strewn about, you may be asking: How long is all this organizing going to take? It depends on how much material you have—the task can be done in anywhere from an hour or less to about four hours. Your documents can be logically organized and neatly placed into your LOK™ by following a few simple guidelines.

First, before beginning to put your documents into a LOK™, sort through them and place them into the categories we have already outlined (see Phases 2 and 3): *Personal Information*, *Medical Documentation*, *Financial Data*, *Legal Records*, and *Community Activities*. (Remember for your LOK™: Make photocopies of all original documents.) This process sets the stage for consolidating material for your LOK™. Second, follow checklists one through five.

Checklist One: Personal Information

- [ ] Social security card
- [ ] Birth certificate (certified copy from the county of record)
- [ ] Passport
- [ ] Naturalization and immigration paperwork (green card, visa, etc.)
- [ ] Driver's license
- [ ] Vehicle registration
- [ ] Vehicle title
- [ ] Business card
- [ ] Company identification card
- [ ] Union card or identification
- [ ] Military identification and applicable paperwork
- [ ] Veterinarian record of services from last visit

There is one document that you obviously cannot include in advance: a death certificate. Death certificates are issued through the county clerk's office, and are usually ordered by a funeral home. There are two types. The first, a certificate with the cause of death, is required for access to any life insurance, supplemental insurance such as from AARP or Blue Cross/Blue Shield, stocks, bonds, pensions, trusts, annuities, CDs or IRA accounts, and checking and savings accounts. Family members will also want a copy for their files. The second type of certificate, without the cause of death, is acceptable for lawyers, real estate transactions (home, condominium or property), condominium associations (copy accepted), motor vehicle departments (copy accepted), and credit card companies (copy accepted).

Checklist Two: Medical Documentation

- [ ] Health insurance card (copies of front and back)
- [ ] Medical insurance policy paperwork (statement of benefits)
- [ ] Medicare plan paperwork
- [ ] Medigap or Medicare supplement policy
  paperwork (statement of benefits)
- [ ] Health care proxy
- [ ] Living will
- [ ] Long-term care insurance policy (statement of benefits)

When my client Sam came to see me, he was not well versed on estate planning, so the ideas of a health care proxy and a living will were new to him. He plugged into the information pretty quickly and learned:

- *With the assistance of an attorney or a specialized software program, you can complete a form along with your estate planning documents in which you designate an individual to act in your stead when you are incapacitated. A health care proxy or health care power of attorney designates a person you choose to direct medical professionals when you are unable to communicate your desires for treatment. When requested, some hospitals provide patients with the form.*

- *A living will instructs your health care proxy and the medical community about how you want to be treated in the event of a medical emergency— for example, whether you choose to undergo surgery, be kept alive on life support, or wish to make an organ donation in the case of your death.*

Checklist Three: Financial Data

- [ ] Year-end statement from each bank account, brokerage account, investment account
- [ ] Most recent tax return
- [ ] Year-end statement for loans and any applicable paperwork (a copy of coupon for payment, etc.)
- [ ] Credit cards (copies of front and back)
- [ ] Real estate property deeds and closing paperwork
- [ ] Appraisals for artwork, jewelry, automobiles, and other collectibles
- [ ] Insurance declaration pages for homeowner's, automobile, umbrella, and personal articles policies; also include any business insurance policies
- [ ] Copy of year-end bill for each ongoing expense (phone, electric, cable, Internet, etc.)
- [ ] Agreements for services (cell phone, landscaping, exterminator, snow removal, housecleaning, etc.)
- [ ] Year-end pay-stub (W-2)
- [ ] Business agreements including registration, filing receipts, and any partnership agreements (include instructions on where to find employee agreements and provide attorney contact information)

Business agreements can be tricky. A close friend, Sarah, shared a story about an uncle who passed away. He was old-fashioned and sealed business deals with a handshake. A person's word is the best form of agreement, he told Sarah. After he died, his wife was confronted with supposed business partners who claimed he owed them money. Since there was no documentation available, attorneys were hired to examine the claims. In the end, the estate settled the claims because there were no signed business agreements to be found and the family wanted to put an end to the legal fees involved in fighting the claims.

Consolidating your financial documents for your LOK™ may help prevent expensive, time-consuming, and frustrating legal snafus.

Checklist Four: Legal Records

- [ ] Prenuptial agreement (do NOT unstaple)
- [ ] Postnuptial agreement (do NOT unstaple)
- [ ] Marriage license
- [ ] Separation agreement
- [ ] Divorce decree
- [ ] Maintenance/child support agreements
- [ ] Adoption paperwork (if international adoption, both in English and from the country of origin)
- [ ] Will (do NOT unstaple)
- [ ] Power of attorney
- [ ] Guardianship
- [ ] Trust
- [ ] Family limited partnership agreement
- [ ] Business partnership agreements
- [ ] Employment agreements

Remember Sam from Checklist Two? He was also clueless about financial powers of attorney, but was clued in promptly about the papers in Checklist Four. Sam understood he needed to include:

- *Power of attorney gives specific powers to another person or persons to sign financial agreements on your behalf in the event you are incapacitated. In instances such as signing a check for a payment, directing brokerage investment accounts, signing a tax return, or completing a real estate transaction, a power of attorney designee can carry on your financial responsibilities when you cannot. The document is best kept with an attorney and released only upon your request or in an emergency situation.*

Sam learned about the two types of powers of attorney:

- *A durable power of attorney immediately transfers powers to a designated person who immediately can execute the power of attorney. This is helpful in the case of an older person or an individual who falls suddenly ill and is in need of a trusted loved one to make important life decisions. A durable power of attorney can be limited to specific circumstances. If you cannot be present to sign, say, real estate documents, you can designate someone to carry out the transaction on your behalf. The person to whom you have granted power would, in this case, be restricted to completing the sale or purchase of that particular property only. Consult your attorney for further details on durable power of attorney.*

- *A springing power of attorney comes into play when you need someone to make legal and medical decisions in your stead because of incapacitation. You need two physicians to acknowledge that you are truly incapacitated and unable to act on your own behalf. In this case, the power of attorney springs into effect when you become unable to express your legal and medical wishes. When discussing estate planning with your attorney, the document is often recommended for everybody, including young people in good health. To find out more, consult your attorney to answer your particular legal questions about springing power of attorney.*

My client Julia came to see me while caring for her dying mother. At the time, her mother was in the hospital and Julia needed access to her accounts in order to pay her mother's bills. She was wrestling with her mother's finances and was having difficulty dealing with the brokerage firm for her mother's accounts. A power of attorney was requested, and Julie had no idea what the document was. I assisted her in contacting her mother's attorney and acquiring the springing power of attorney document her mother had filed with him so Julia could keep her mother's financial health intact. For Julia that meant she could assure that her mom received the appropriate daily care.

Guardianship papers also appoint an individual to oversee the daily physical care of an infirm person. Guardianship papers quell disputes that may arise over whom responsibility falls to. You want to avoid guardianship judgments that can take up to several weeks and require a court hearing, along with attorney expenses. Ask your estate attorney whether guardianship papers are required in your state. An attorney can execute the document along with your will and other estate planning papers.

Because of the round-the-clock care that Julia's mother needed, Julia was tied up at the hospital and unable to leave town for a real estate transaction. She then assigned durable power of attorney to a friend located near the closing, and was able to purchase the property without having to travel out of state.

Checklist Five: Community Activities

- [ ] *Baptismal certificate*
- [ ] *Confirmation certificate*
- [ ] *Networking or professional group agreements*
- [ ] *Health or fitness club agreements for services*
- [ ] *Social club agreements*
- [ ] *Copies from your Rolodex, PDA, electronic organizer, or address book of important contact people (who they are and how they are affiliated with you)*

Once you have copies of these papers, you are halfway through the document hunt necessary for completing your LOK™. Take a short break and relax for a few moments before continuing the journey.

Check Out Your Documents

Copies of all your important documents go in your LOK™. It is impractical to include originals, such as your driver's license or company identification card, as you may use them every day. Many institutions and organizations do require original documents, so your loved ones will need to know where to find those. To provide clarification and eliminate guessing games for the ones you love, make copies and originals accessible.

To better assist you with organizing your documents, go to *www.TheLOK.com*.

Download the LOK Documents Workbook™. Let it be your guide in the final throes of getting your paperwork together. If you are building a hard copy LOK™, print out the files and follow the instructions for creating lists and referencing materials. If you are working on an electronic LOK™, your scanned documents and a list of locations where to find the originals can be saved to your computer.

Check In with Your LOK

The documents in the checklists above not only identify your immediate world but also are indispensable in an emergency situation. The paperwork ranges from your birth certificate and driver's license to company identification cards and military papers. Do you have photocopies of all the items on the *Personal* Identification checklist? Follow the list of documents in the checklist and start putting your copies into the kit. Remember to include (as the first document in the kit) an index detailing where the originals are stored; the first page summarizes what

you have in the section and where the originals are. Follow the same guidelines for organizing your paperwork into the *Medical, Financial, Legal, and Community* sections of your LOK™.Use the LOK Documents Workbook™ to help you stay organized.

Order from Chaos

Gathering the items from the checklists and putting them together in one accessible place reduces the chaos your loved ones experience when your and their worlds are turned upside down. Think of your efforts this way: Knowing that you have critical documents organized for the ones you love means you can breathe a little easier. Locking up your documents in a tidy package may create a prolonged sigh of relief. So live with passion—but document it! The time spent building a LOK™ will be rewarded multifold.

Phase

5

Key To Your Connections

*Put together the
ultimate contact list...*

A s we explore the world and have new experiences, we form a "life team" or support network made up of people whom we count on for assistance and enjoyment. Our team is ready to lend a helping hand and helps us when we need guidance. Imagine something unexpected happens to you, and you can't communicate with your team. Who would step up to assist the ones you love in helping you?

Phase 5 empowers you to compile the ultimate contact list as a blueprint of your life. You create an extraordinary address book, which provides you and your loved ones with a quick and easy reference to the people who are there for you every step of the way as you venture forth in the world.

The worksheets for this section prompt you to give details about the important people in your life and provide information about the best way to reach them. You build step by step a list of people for your team so loved ones won't need to pour through address books, Rolodexes, Palm Pilots, BlackBerries, or anything else to access an important contact number or e-mail address.

Mission Possible

Your task is to put together all the contact information puzzle pieces for your team. As you look at the materials that you have gathered for your LOK™, you may find you have people's contact information all over the place—scribbled on many pieces of paper, printed on business cards, handwritten in notebooks, etc. Create a detailed list of the people in your life and their whereabouts.

Start with the hard copy information you have on hand. Set aside your address books, Rolodexes, business card binders, miscellaneous contact lists, and statements (from insurance companies, financial institutions, credit card companies, and monthly bills).

Where do you keep contact information? Microsoft Outlook is an example of a program that stores lots of contact details. Do you use a PDA, such as a Palm Pilot or electronic organizer, or a cell phone directory, or e-mail account to stay in touch? (Remember, when dealing in the digital world, you may want to compile a list of your user-names and passwords in the event your loved ones need access to your information.) Is your information kept at both your home and office? Do you have Post-It Notes® stuck to your desk, telephone, or computer? Contact information is extremely valuable for your LOK™, so be sure to get it together before you move on.

Forward Motion

I have created a user-friendly workbook for you to consolidate information about your contacts. Whether you fill in the data electronically or write it all down on a printed sheet, the LOK Contact List Workbook™ speeds you through the process. Please go to www.TheLOK.com to download the LOK Contact List Workbook™ .

Get Ready to Boogie!

Recognize that you have an awesome organization system built into the LOK™. The LOK Contact List Workbook™ will help you sort out your *Personal, Medical, Financial, Legal,* and *Community* contacts too. For each category of the LOK™ include precise data for each contact: the name and your association with the contact—family, friend, employment, business or career, pet related, financial, recreational, etc. Record the contact's mailing address, street address, telephone numbers (home, office, cell phone), fax number, and e-mail address (home and business). Follow the fill-in-the-blank format of the LOK Contact List Workbook™ as you breeze through the data.

Getting Personal

Designate a family member, next of kin, or close friend as an emergency contact. In the United States, firefighters and paramedics are trained to look in your cell phone for the name of a person to contact in case of emergency (ICE). Add an ICE entry to your cell phone directory. List in your LOK Contact List Workbook™ additional people in your immediate family, including spouse, parents, children, grandparents, siblings, or other relatives, as well as good friends. Jot down close neighbors whom you speak with on a regular basis and who may have that extra key to your apartment.

Work contacts also belong in the *Personal* contact information. Include the name of your boss, a human resources person, payroll and pension contacts, and a close coworker or colleague.

Got contacts in the military or in the union? Provide information for the main offices and key individuals in the organization, such as a commanding officer, union representative, benefits person, or insurance expert. People—on or off the job—remain the most valuable resources in times of trouble.

An additional consideration for the *Personal* category: Do you own property and rent out space to a tenant? Your tenant belongs on your contact list. If you live in a co-operative apartment building or condominium complex, or if you rent an apartment, be sure to include the name and contact information for the superintendent and the key individuals from the property management or condominium association for the building.

Companies and service providers, such as electric, telephone, cell phone, cable, Internet, landscaper or gardener, cleaning person or housekeeper, handyman, etc., need to be part of your *Personal* contact information. Knowing contact information will save loved ones lots of grief and frustration when attempting, for example, to address the upkeep of your household so it is in good condition when you return. In the event of death, loved ones need access to this kind of information in order to stop services so your accounts don't go into arrears. If service providers have keys or access codes to enter your property or home, loved ones will be able to retrieve keys and change locks or digital codes to keep your property safe and secure.

Do you have people who take care of your pet? Make these resources quick and easy for your loved ones to find so your pet continues to receive attention and love in your absence. When making your list, think veterinarian, dog walker, cat sitter, pet groomer, kennel contacts, and pet food store (include the foods your pet generally eats).

Do you consult personal advisors such as mentors, coaches, spiritual advisors, religious advisors (priest, rabbi, imam, or minister), or astrologers? Put these people in your *Personal* contact list too.

Check in with the LOK Contact List Workbook™ and use it as a reference for keeping all your information in order. Another reminder: If you have various online accounts with different user names and passwords, create a list of log-on information.

Taking Care

Who takes care of your mind and body? Health practitioners' information sometimes falls though the cracks. Gather the *Medical* contact information you have from business cards, address books, office stationery, or referrals and put the names, addresses, and phone numbers in one master list. Start by listing your primary medical doctor, gynecologist, medical specialist for chronic conditions, dermatologist, dentist, and other. The other category consists of specialists who support your overall good health, including your nutritionist, psychologist, chiropractor, acupuncturist, Reiki practitioner, massage therapist, physical therapist, personal trainer, etc. Include individuals whom you have visited within the last twelve months. If you haven't been to a doctor, dentist, or other healthcare practitioner in quite some time, include the contact information for the last medical professional you saw.

Give details: Record your health insurance, such as medical and hospitalization policies (number and date of contract), and reference any long-term care policies. If you have a health insurance agent, be sure to include his name and telephone number and contact information for the health insurance company. Do you use a personal aid or the services of an assistance agency, such as a visiting nurse service or another private organization? Remember to include the agency office contact information and names of individuals who provide care for you on a regular basis.

Money Tree

Most people have a money tree of sorts—a network of interrelating financial experts who service their finances. Try categorizing people into areas of expertise so your loved ones can cull through the list and locate instantly the person they need to speak with. List all the *Financial* contacts who tend your money garden. Begin with your LOK Specialist™, financial planner or advisor, and your accountant. They are the roots of your financial team. These individuals will direct your loved ones to the other financial experts on your team.

Let's take a look at your banking and investment relationships. Record the names and contact information for the various institutions as well as the numbers on each account, such as your checking and savings, investment, and so on. Include lending institutions and credit card company information, mortgage company contacts, student loan information, any transportation loans (car, boat, motorcycle) or leased vehicles, aircraft leasing, or other loans you may have. Do you have loans for your business or real estate investment ventures? Keep all loan numbers for promissory accounts on file.

What about business relationships you have with real estate brokers, appraisers, general contractors, construction company contacts, home-owner's associations (condominiums and gated communities), co-op boards, superintendents, and property management company contacts? These people belong on your contact lists, as do the names and addresses for insurance agents for your property and businesses. Be specific.

If you own and operate a business, list all contact information for quick and easy reference. Incorporate data about your business partners, key staff, clients, and vendors. If something unexpected happens to you, your loved ones can jump in to keep your business on track. Having access to information about your business and the clients you have developed a relationship with over the years will help loved ones sustain the business in your stead. A simple list of vendor contacts, for example, can make maintaining your business easy; vendors can be paid in full so your company's credit rating doesn't suffer while you are on the mend. When you return to the business, you can plug back into these relationships; in the meantime your clients and vendors feel that they have been well informed and will want to assist you in your time of need.

Any other considerations for list making? Consult the LOK Contact List Workbook™ and let it guide you through the process.

Legal Lineup

Your *Legal* team primarily consists of attorneys. The LOK Contact List Workbook™ helps you to compile their contact information based on their legal expertise. The following is a short list of areas of expertise in which you may have enlisted experts in the law: personal, estate, elder law, real estate, matrimonial, business or corporate, adoption, or immigration. In addition, include the name of any assistant, paralegal, or other contact in your lawyer's office whom you speak with on a regular basis.

Community Appeal

Is your extended community vast and unwieldy? The *Community* category maps your interactions and activities, and tracks your extended family members and friends. These community contacts are relatives (your aunts, uncles, and cousins), friends, and acquaintances—those who are not in your innermost circle but whom you want informed of important changes in your life. They may include people you have met overseas on vacation, or neighbors and friends you see from time to time at a second home at the beach.

Give some thought to your religious affiliations and the church, temple, or mosque where you interact with groups and communities. Are you on any boards or committees? Select a few key people within these organizations whom your loved ones can contact regarding your condition or notification of death.

Do you participate in ongoing special interest or networking groups? In your list of *Community* contacts, provide the name and type of group (from nonprofit organizations to charity groups and fundraising), your participation, and contact information for a group leader with whom your loved ones can communicate.

Good *Community* contacts to fill into your LOK Contact List Workbook™ include health and fitness clubs, social groups (poker, bridge, or canasta), ballroom dancing groups, baseball, bowling, other team sports, motorcycle or cycling clubs, etc. Make note also of the classes, workshops, and courses you are enrolled in so that loved ones can cancel them if necessary.

And not to be overlooked: Many people accumulate frequent flyer miles and reward points. In the LOK Contact List Workbook™ be sure to include the name and number on all frequent flyer accounts. Points and rewards may be transferred to family members in the event of an emergency situation or death of the account holder. Married women often use their maiden names on the accounts, or in the case of a divorce, their married name may still be on record.

Loving Kindness

Take a bow. You have sorted, sifted, and consolidated a plethora of contact information into the ultimate contact list. Your loved ones will thank you kindly; now they have only one central place to look—your LOK™.

An old popular song goes: "Lift up your fellow man, lend him a helping hand—put a little love in your heart…" The sheer number of people that sustain us is hard to fathom—but there they are, listed by name and contact information, in our LOK™. The people in your life make the journey rich and rewarding. Honor them, and enjoy and share your gratitude. Be grateful for their presence, tremendous support, and assistance as they extend their loving kindness during an emergency or time of great need.

My mantra: Loving kindness and assistance are eternally welcomed and appreciated.

6

Un-LOK Your Life

*Let your
loved ones in...*

In the event you become incapacitated and cannot communicate, are your loved ones aware of how full your life is? They may not be fully aware of the extent of your passions and life journey—how rich, full of beauty and inspiration, your life truly is. Let's investigate your life experiences, which are infinitely more interesting than examining documents, data, company ID cards, and insurance policies.

Phase 6 is the place to let your life and love shine. This is the time to share who you truly are so you can communicate compassionately and effectively. Allow your loved ones to be party to your unique life. There are a multitude of activities you engage in and purposeful ways you spend your time that your loved ones want to know about in your LOK™.

Through the Looking Glass

Think of the LOK™ as a looking glass: it reflects subjective information about who you are—your values, passions, beliefs, and experiences. If you were unable to communicate fully with your loved ones, what would you want them to know about you? Would you have them look at your writing, art, journals and diaries, scrapbooks, poetry, favorite books; tell them about films that changed your life; share stories about the wondrous places you've been; let them know about your courageous volunteer efforts and the charities to which you contribute? The ones you love can peer into your LOK™ and learn about your life. Perhaps there are special messages you would want your loved ones to learn in the event something unexpected happens to you. Are there specific instructions not appropriate to include in your will or other estate planning documents that you want to leave for loved ones in the event of your death?

Clear Communication

Subjective personal information about yourself can be more difficult to pin down than documents and papers, contact information, and forms of identification. Do you record experiences and moments that have inspired, transformed, and expanded your life perspective? Mementos may include a photograph of a much-loved infant, a poem you wrote for a special occasion, or diaries you have kept since you were little—a day-by-day emotional and intellectual transcript of your life. If you're a musician, your experiences may be reflected through the music you write and record. If you're a painter or artist, the works you create are a spiritual blueprint of your life.

The following list reflects modes of expression to share your life journey. Which of these are you most inclined to use to record meaningful or inspiring life events? Next to each item jot down whether the style of communication resonates well with your own. Take a few moments to think about it. If you would like to explore a new method of recording your life experiences, include it here too:

Photographs:

Diaries:

Writing journals:

Drawing journals:

Paintings:

Sculpture:

Video/film:

Music—lyrics and/or compositions:

Scrapbooks:

Voice recordings:

Home videos:

Blogs:

Other:

To assist you in your experimentation, respond to the following: When something extraordinary happens to you, how do you record the moment? For example, if you meet a celebrity, do you ask someone to take a picture? Do you make home videos of your baby daughter? Maybe you write love songs. Did you write your own wedding vows? Do you keep a diary or journal?

Playback

When Kathy travels to a far-flung destination she collects lots of pictures, postcards, pamphlets, and souvenirs. She returns home and compiles everything into a scrapbook. Carefully pasting pictures, souvenirs, and typed comments into pages in a fabric-covered bound book with the vacation destination and dates embroidered on the cover, Kathy celebrates her trip, the places she has been, and the people who have shared the experience.

Duncan also has a desire to document his experiences. As a painter, he enjoys traveling and hiking. When he hikes, Duncan takes photographs

of different perspectives from mountaintops and later paints from the photographs. His paintings, oil on canvas, are exhibited in his studio and in art galleries. Through artwork Duncan records his life.

Do you share your photo albums and writing of your journeys with nearest and dearest? If a catastrophe happened and you were seriously injured or killed, would you want your loved ones to find these memories? How else can they appreciate the life you have led and the experiences you have enjoyed?

Where one person likes to shoot video of family and friends, another person may prefer journal writing. What are the materials you use to record your life? How will you capture the moments of your life? Identify your personal style of recording your life and think about how to share your journey with the ones you love. Feel free to visit www.TheLOK.com and download The Love in a LOK Workbook™.

Express Yourself

There is a way to open the door and let your loved ones in. What are your favorite places, foods, drinks, sports, performing arts, musicians and bands, films, television programs, books, poems, and sayings?

Note your responses. Make a collage. Spend an hour cutting out pictures from magazines that reflect your life experiences. Gluing images and found art on paper is a fun activity to do with children too. You can learn a lot about yourself and the kids from the process. Think about creating a series of collages—do one a year as testimony to your evolving life. If your collages are on 8 1/2" x 11" construction paper, they may fit right in your LOK™.

There are, of course, other forms of playback. Diane is a videographer who shoots corporate events for large companies. In her free time she travels, spends time with friends, dines at trendy restaurants, and sees movies regularly. In a diary format, she records her life and activities on video: the exotic places she has been, shots of Indian and Chinese cuisine, excerpts from her favorite movie *My Big Fat Greek Wedding*, and life at home with her cat Figaro.

Some people choose poetry to express themselves. When my grandfather passed away, our family celebrated his legacy and work ethic in a short poem he wrote:

> *If a job is once begun,*
> *never leave it 'til it's done.*
> *Be its master, great or small.*
> *Do it well or not at all.*
> —Abraham "Al" Wilkov

What are your passions? What drives your life? What activities are you engaged in that define who you really are, say, volunteering at the local soup kitchen or reading bedtime stories to children at the local shelter?

Janine, for example, anonymously funds college educations for children of low-income families, while her brother Carmine is passionate about social change and donates money and time to organizations addressing problems of AIDS, cancer, the environment, wildlife, hunger, and poverty.

Some people give their time and money to churches or schools, while others donate to charities. Share how you participate in the world with a note in your LOK™. Think of your missive as a means to tipping off loved ones to what is important in your world. Let them know the details of your activities and contributions to the community so they may continue your legacy. For additional guidance refer to the Love in the LOK Workbook™.

Contemplation Time

Death and dying bring up thoughts and feelings about how we live. Some go to great lengths to avoid discussions of death. Most of us never think about passing from this life. We don't think much about dying until a loved one passes away. A death in the family may encourage us to ponder our own life plan and reflect on our mortality. Some of us think very deeply about our own passing. A few are concerned with how we will be remembered and how the community pays tribute to us. In light of this, I urge you to reflect on this: If you passed away today, what would your obituary say?

When my grandmother died, my family sat down and read the previous day's obituaries in the newspaper. Some of the obituaries included pictures, names of spouses, children, grandchildren, etc. Many families asked for donations to be sent to specific charities on behalf of the beloved deceased. Our family discussed the obituaries that inspired us. We kept asking: How would Grandmother want us to commemorate her?

What would you want your obit to say? Rebecca's best friend Stephanie was killed in a car accident at age 32. When Rebecca recovered from the initial shock of losing her friend, she was asked by Stephanie's family to read the obituary they had written before it was published. Rebecca enjoyed reading the thoughtful write-up of her friend's life; the obit captured Stephanie's inner beauty. Reading it brightened Rebecca's mood—one sentence about Stephanie's pets, two dwarf hamsters who liked to play fetch with tiny sticks, made her giggle and brought tears to her eyes too. What Rebecca didn't know was that Stephanie had written her own obituary a year earlier as an exercise and had included it in her LOK™. Stephanie wanted her obit to be funny and playful; her family used her draft to write the final obituary submitted to the newspaper.

Sound strange? I encourage you to take some time and write your own obituary. Think about how you see yourself, how others see you, and the message you would like to leave behind. Look through the papers for examples. When you have completed the exercise, place it into your LOK™. Remember you can return to the exercise at another time to update the information.

A eulogy, literally "good words," commemorates the deceased's life. Have you ever listened closely to a eulogy at a service? Think back: Did relatives and loved ones read special passages from writing, favorite poems, or show art as a tribute to the departed? Maybe you listened to a pastor or rabbi read passages from the scriptures. Maybe you heard a son describe the times he spent playing catch with his dad or the meaningful father-and-son talks they shared.

At the beginning of the film *Love Actually*, a woman passes away and at her funeral her husband plays a slide show accompanied by the Bay City Rollers' "Bye Bye Baby." This is a different take on the traditional funeral eulogy.

Like the obit exercise, try writing a eulogy—it can be your own or for someone you love. How would you like your eulogy to sound? The exercise is not meant to be morbid but transformational. The aim is to inspire you—celebrate what you have accomplished. In the process, you may become more discerning and selective; you learn to pinpoint activities, interests, and passions you want to pursue and ignore those that don't really hold much meaning.

Ready to try? Sit down at your desk or computer and write a eulogy in, say, fifteen minutes. Set a timer and focus on the task at hand. Once you are done, read it out loud or to someone you love. You can also ask a loved one to read it back to you. The exercise will encourage you to reflect differently on your life.

The rabbi at both my grandfather's and, recently, my grandmother's funerals shared a wonderful anonymous poem called "The Measure of a Man":

> Not "How did he die?" But "How did he live?"
> Not "What did he gain?" But "What did he give?"
> Not "What was his station?" But "Had he a heart?"
> And "How did he play his God-given part?"
> Not "What was his shrine?" Nor "What was his creed?"
> But "Had he befriended those really in need?"
> Not "What did the piece in the newspaper say?"
> But "How many were sorry when he passed away?"
> Was he ever ready with a word or good cheer,
> To bring back a smile, to banish a tear?
> These are the units to measure the worth
> Of a man as a man, regardless of birth.

In addition to sharing your favorite poetry selections, perhaps you want to leave specific instructions on what to do with your body when you die (burial, cremation, donating body parts to science). If you don't feel a need to decide what happens to your body when you die, you may care more about how your spirit is left intact.

A video recording keeps alive the spirit of the dearly departed. A great-grandchild can experience his ancestors through film and video recordings. Relatives can share their lives on camera—be silly and make funny facial expressions that we know and love. A granddaughter can experience the tone and tempo of her grandmother's voice, how she spoke and gesticulated. On film a husband still can appreciate the loving way his beautiful bride regarded him on their wedding day.

Extrasensory Perception

Star in your own video: Record yourself and share your life story. Video is a great way for loved ones to preserve your memory and feel close to you forever; it lets loved ones in on your unique insights. Hold up

photographs of events and people in your life journey. Lead your audience to know you on a deeper level. This process is an opportunity at any age to welcome others into your life. Share the love.

Leave a metaphorical trail of breadcrumbs, as in *Hansel and Gretel*, so loved ones can trace the paths you have traveled. Don't hold back—share everything: your triumphs, sorrows, heroic actions, and the moments you wish no one really knew about. If you don't share, who will?

Memories are the greatest gifts you can give. Leave behind a dazzling treasure chest filled with abundant riches: your collages, scrapbooks, journals, diaries, music, art, photography, and recordings LOK'd in forever.

Phase

7

Use It

*Focus on an
Action Plan...*

*I*f you have been reading this book attentively and still haven't gotten
started on your LOK™, I encourage you to begin today. Life happens
and freak occurrences cannot be predicted. When catastrophe
strikes, the LOK™ becomes a tremendous gift because it contains top-
secret contact information with a personal twist. It's a powerful tool
that may save the day or your life. When loved ones find information
immediately accessible in a LOK™; they can turn their attention to you
and your comfort and safety. In Phase 7, you witness how the LOK™
springs into action.

Safe and Sound

Your LOK™ contains copies of your important documents for a simple
reason: If your LOK™ falls into the wrong hands, the original material
is safe. A startling statistic from the 2006 Identity Fraud Survey Report,
conducted by the Council of Better Business Bureaus and the Javelin
Strategy & Research company, states that nearly half (47 percent) of
all identity theft is perpetrated by someone the victim knows. It could
be a friend, neighbor, family member, or other acquaintance. Another
interesting statistic from the same source is that Generation Xers (ages
25-34) experience the highest rate of identity theft, ahead of Baby
Boomers and the 65-and-up groups. The kit is not intended as a calling
card for predators to run away with victims' vital information.

Whether you use a hard copy or electronic LOK™, be mindful of
where you store it and where the originals are. In short, your LOK™
needs to be accessible in an emergency situation so your loved ones can
get to it, but secure to prevent easy access by predators.

A LOK Specialist™ asks that you identify primary and secondary
persons to access your information in emergencies. In case your loved
ones cannot find your kit, your LOK Specialist™ has backup.

Critical Care

In the heat of an emergency, people with the best intentions do not always have the information on hand to make careful decisions. The LOK™ provides a plan of action, emergency instruction that integrates your loved ones. The plan allows your appointed people full access to documents, personal information, and vital statistics so they can administer your care. The roles and responsibilities of your Core Team™ are mapped out in the LOK™. When disaster strikes, you are fully supported physically, emotionally, financially, and spiritually because emergency scenarios have been anticipated and planned for.

When catastrophes occur, your loved ones can consult the kit for vital information before springing into action. The focus remains on you—and getting the best care or help—instead of inviting chaos into everybody's lives. With a LOK™, stress and frustration are greatly reduced for loved ones, who can work together effectively in crisis mode and tend to your needs.

The Core Team

Define carefully the roles and responsibilities of your Core Team™ based on geographic location and strengths. Your brother who lives on the other side of the country is excellent with your finances. Geographic location won't affect his role as the person in charge of administering your money. Your best friends live locally and have room in their homes and hearts to care for your children if necessary. The kit assigns day-to-day responsibilities to trusted individuals beyond playing their role as a person named in an estate plan. Some people who play key roles in your LOK™ emergency plan are also players in your estate planning. For assistance in selecting who's who on your Core Team™ refer to www.TheLOK.com and download My Core Team Worksheet™. Use the worksheet (or make your own) to assign people to the following roles (if you have a small family and just a handful of close friends you can combine roles, with one person filling two or three positions in a pinch):

1. *Emergency Contact. This is the person you have placed in your cell phone under "ICE." He or she provides vital information in the event your identification, money, and other important items are lost or stolen. In addition, this person contacts emergency workers such as paramedics, police, firefighters, or a hospital in the event you have an accident. Familiar with the other members on your Core Team™, this designated point person is responsible for notifying the others on your team.*

2. *Data Provider. The person to whom you entrust full access to your LOK™ knows where the kit is stored and how to access it quickly. With pre-approval to enlist the assistance of your LOK Specialist™, the data provider may also double as your emergency contact.*

3. *Healthcare Proxy or Power of Attorney. An individual or individuals you name in your estate planning documents to direct medical professionals in your care should you be unable to communicate. If you have not begun your estate planning, seek out an attorney and get started.*

4. *Power of Attorney. Person or persons whom you have asked to pay your bills and attend to your financial transactions in the event that you are incapacitated.*

5. *Primary Caretaker. The primary caretaker's focus is to secure your safety and welfare: for example, ride with you in an ambulance to the*

hospital or accompany you from an accident or crime scene. If you are already en route to a hospital, the primary person may be the first to arrive and provide information (your identification, vital statistics, and medical history).

6. *Guardian. The guardian's role is to take care of legal dependents: children, elderly parents, or other disabled or dependent persons who rely on you. In the event you pass away, a guardian is named in your estate documents.*

7. *Pet Caretaker. The pet caretaker takes care of your beloved pet when something unexpected happens to you. Your dog, cat, fish, birds, hamsters, and so on need food, water, a clean place to sleep, and a waste disposal plan. A pet caretaker is authorized to contact your veterinarian should your pet require boarding or kenneling while you are on the mend. Consider assigning the role to multiple helpers. Depending on where you and your pet(s) are based, consider naming a pet caretaker who can adopt your friend in case of death. Don't be shy: Include your pet in your estate planning.*

8. *Residence Caretaker. Charged with the care and upkeep of your home, the residence caretaker coordinates the household resources: housecleaner, landscaper, exterminator, etc. Words of practical wisdom: select someone who lives nearby.*

When disastrous situations unfold, the Core Team™ comes together to support you. Communicate in advance with all parties about the role you would like them to play. Make sure everybody is committed to you and your loved ones before naming them in your LOK™.

LEAP into Action

When I was a young girl in the 1970s, I was introduced to my first emergency plan. At the time, advertisements on television spoke about creating a family plan in case of fire. Home fire drills became common practice; establishing and rehearsing an emergency plan was routine. Loved ones were taught how to get out of a burning house and where to meet afterwards. Once family members reached safe haven, they verified that everyone had made it out.

Many assume that their loved ones, out of obligation and love, will automatically step up to the plate. Now that your kit is ready for action and you have established a Core Team™, have tryouts. Practice what each individual does in a crisis. Isn't it empowering to go over an emergency plan with the ones you love before a catastrophe?

Subscribing to a Life Emergency Assistance Plan™ (LEAP™) means your systems are in place and your team is good to go. When your "fire drill" turns real, your loved ones are ready for action. The following examples illustrate situations during which your Core Team™ comes together with your LOK™ to overcome obstacles:

Situation #1 – Identity Theft

Janice, 28, was applying for her first mortgage for an apartment in Chicago. The young professional was prepared and excited about becoming a homeowner; she had been saving diligently for her down payment, and at last had the required amount. The mortgage broker sadly informed Janice that she was denied the money because of a low credit score; she had too many credit lines in relation to her income. Janice only owned only two credit cards, whose monthly balances she always paid promptly. The mortgage broker then provided a complimentary credit report. The young professional learned that someone had been opening charge accounts in her name for what appeared to be over three months. Each credit line was maxed out, and the balances were carried over from month to month. She did not recognize the address where those statements were sent. Unnerved, she immediately contacted the police and informed them that she was a victim of identity theft.

The information and documents the police department needed to file the report were in Janice's LOK™. Janice got lucky: in a time of chaos, frustration, and anger, she didn't have to look far and wide for information.

Situation #2 – Theft: International and Domestic

Madeline was traveling from the United States to Europe. In London, she jumped on the underground railway system, the "Tube," to skip across town to Hyde Park. Exiting the train at her stop, she reached into her pocketbook for her sunglasses and noticed that her wallet, with passport, money, and itinerary, had been taken. Theft occurs when you are thousands of miles from home, or right in your own backyard.

Madeline called her ICE Contact and sister Rebecca about the situation. Then, she reported the crime to Scotland Yard. Needing assistance with the British questionnaire, she contacted George, her Critical Data Provider and best friend. George accessed her LOK™ in New York and faxed a copy of Madeline's passport to Scotland Yard and to the U.S. Embassy in London so she could acquire a new passport. George called Madeline and provided her with her banker Sam's contact information, the customer service numbers for each credit card, and the credit card numbers, expiration dates, and security codes on the back of the cards. Madeline then contacted the companies directly to notify them of the theft and order replacement cards. Lastly, George faxed an additional photocopy of her passport to her hotel and wired some money through Western Union.

Madeline's safety, wellbeing, and financial recovery overseas were taken care of in a few hours because Madeline had taken the time to put together a LOK™.

Situation #3 – Accidents and Injuries

Accidents happen—just ask Jonathan from Boston. He is a skier whose dream is to ski every high peak in North America as well as to ski the most exclusive mountains in Switzerland and Italy. Not too long ago, he and some friends were in Steamboat Springs, Colorado, on their semiannual ski adventure, when an out-of-control skier crashed into Jonathan, dragging him off the main slope. Rammed into a small tree, he broke his leg and knee in three places. His ski buddies saw the whole incident unfold; they watched incredulously as a stranger knocked Jonathan out for the count. The friends immediately contacted the ski patrol, who got Jonathan down the mountain and to a hospital.

Because Jonathan and his group of ski buddies had a LEAP™, the men were able to spring into action on behalf of their friend. The ski resort and police department wanted a report filed on the incident so Tom took care of this. Tom also contacted Steve, Jonathan's domestic partner, because Steve is Jonathan's ICE Contact and his Critical Data Provider. Tom asked Steve for health information from Jonathan's LOK™. Steve pulled out copies of Jonathan's driver's license, health insurance information card, medical contact numbers, and medical information, including Jonathan's recent diagnosis of type 2 diabetes. While Tom took care of these details, Brian jumped into the ambulance with Jonathan and accompanied him to the hospital. Tom provided the hospital with the information it required to admit Jonathan and get him immediate attention. Steve faxed copies of documents from Jonathan's LOK™ to the hospital administration. Within a few hours of Jonathan's accident, the ski group had calmly addressed the calamity. The next day, Steve arrived to support Jonathan in his recovery and remind him gently how Jonathan ought to take up fishing instead of skiing!

A Core Team™ that moves without further ado through difficult situations is a blessing. Taking the time to put together and discuss your LEAP™ is key. For example, before you go on a two-week vacation or participate in a cycling race, decide upon a LEAP™, a contingency plan, just in case.

Situation #4 – Emergency Room Care

Martha, 40, and her husband Joel, 45, dined one Saturday night in the latest restaurant in their suburban Chicago neighborhood. They and two other couples regularly shared dinner dates, and the group knew that there was always the remote possibility that the food would be awful.

Once, someone in the group had suffered food poisoning. One night toward the end of a spectacular meal, Martha wasn't feeling well. She became dizzy, light-headed, and nauseated.

What was happening to Martha?

As they would later discover, her appendix burst an hour before they met for dinner. As a result of the highly toxic fluids in her body, Martha felt faint and doubled over in pain.

"Misfortune arises when we least expect it."

The friends looked to Joel—the ICE Contact for his wife. Joel asked Larry to call 911, then telephoned his 16-year-old son Paul who was at home and asked him to grab Martha's purse and come to the restaurant with Larry (who was on his way to pick up the teen). Paul was also asked to call Charles, the Data Provider, to access Martha's LOK™ for primary doctor's contact information and provide a list of her prescription medicine and healthcare supplements. (Providing information to the paramedics and the hospital saved Martha's life because the medical teams were more easily able to eliminate reasons Martha had fallen ill.)

Joel rode in the ambulance with Martha to the hospital. Joel had Paul call Martha's mother to ask her to meet them at the hospital too. Larry, after dropping Paul off at the hospital, returned to the house to walk Martha's dog and give the pet water and food.

Situations like this happen every day to people. Sometimes misfortune arises when we're halfway around the world on a business trip, honeymoon, or adventure vacation to the remote Amazon wilds. Your LOK™ is one of your best friends in a disaster; in the hands of your team players it offers protection and restores calm.

Are you and your loved ones prepared to take action during a calamity?

Situation #5 – Geriatrics

Lorraine's mother Celeste is 80 years old. Leonard, Celeste's husband of fifty-one years, recently passed away. Celeste's health has been pretty good except for the occasional aches and pains. The octogenarian does line dancing and water aerobics twice a week at the senior living community in Phoenix where she resides. In short Celeste is happy and active, living a fulfilling life with friends, children, and grandchildren.

Celeste and Leonard had purchased a long-term care insurance policy and updated their estate planning documents with an elder law attorney before Leonard's death. They made the changes to the wills and filed the documents. Life went on in their beautiful home in Scottsdale, Arizona.

When Leonard was diagnosed with first stages of lung cancer, Lorraine and her brother and sister became equally concerned about Celeste. Lorraine lives in California. Her brother Phil lives in South Carolina, and their sister Katherine lives in London. Leonard's care required many treatments, and Celeste cared for him on her own with occasional help from Lorraine and Katherine. Phil checked in with his parents every other week and had them speak with Katie, their five-year-old granddaughter. Celeste used a car service and a part-time personal aid to bring Leonard to the hospital. Leonard's disease advanced quickly, and within eight months of his diagnosis he passed away.

After grieving for months, Celeste once again updated her documents with the elder law attorney. She decided to remain in her home of twenty years. A family meeting was called. Lorraine wanted to establish how the siblings would care for their mother should an unexpected event occur with Celeste who was living in a large house on her own. How would the children, none of whom lived in Arizona, support and care for their mom? With Lorraine in San Francisco and the other siblings living more than eight hours away by plane from their mom, Lorraine wanted to have a LEAP™ in place should Celeste, say, fall, break a bone, or need medical assistance.

Celeste felt her children needn't worry. Lorraine was particularly concerned because she had recently witnessed a close friend who lived through a nightmare when her mother unexpectedly fell ill. The mother had been in great health too, and was also living alone in the family home after her husband passed away. Lorraine watched week by week the saga of her friend's chaotic existence. Flying constantly back and forth between San Francisco and Texas, Lorraine's friend was having a tough time assisting her mother while working full time and taking care of her own children. But Phil, Lorraine's brother, agreed with Celeste: "Mom is doing great. Why do we have to discuss this now?"

Lorraine persisted. She wanted to establish a LEAP™ right away in case of an emergency. Celeste already had a LOK™, which she had agreed to build with Lorraine a year before Leonard died. Who could the siblings trust locally to assist Celeste in an emergency? The children contacted a few of the younger neighbors and were able to enlist their help as members of Celeste's Emergency Assistance Team.

Celeste was a very private person and didn't enjoy discussing the details of her life with anyone, including her children. Lorraine and her siblings would all have to become Lorraine's ICE Contacts and Data Providers. They also needed to know how she paid her bills, and where her original documents were kept.

Six months later, Celeste slipped and fell on the tennis court and broke her hip and elbow. The pain was so intense that Celeste went into shock and passed out. Her tennis partner Marie got immediate assistance from the tennis club personnel. The tennis pro remembered

Celeste's conversation about her LOK™ and how her daughter insisted that her contact information remain on file at the club in the event of an emergency. He promptly called Lorraine and notified her of the accident. Lorraine made phone calls to her mother's friend and neighbor, Judith, who was named in Celeste's LOK™ as the primary person on the scene, whose job it was to remain with and assist Celeste until a family member could get there. Judith would stay with Celeste at the hospital in Scottsdale until Lorraine arrived.

Lorraine knew that her mother was allergic to specific medications that paramedics typically use in emergency situations like this one. When the paramedics pulled into the club, the tennis pro called back Lorraine, who, with a copy of her mom's LOK™ at her disposal, was able to provide all the necessary medical information. The LEAP™ proved invaluable: The chaos factor was reduced because Celeste's team was there for her.

Situation #6 – Death

As Rosalie's eldest child, Kevin led the family in the settlement of their mother's estate. Before her health declined, Kevin put together a LOK™ for his mom because he didn't know where her legal and financial documents were, nor did he have names and contact information for her estate planning lawyer or other financial professionals. Additionally, Kevin wanted to record her telling stories about her life on video.

Mother and son chose Rick in Santa Fe as their LOK Specialist™. Kevin hadn't completed his own estate plan, so he was grateful to Rick for expediting the kit process. "At first, Mom resisted giving detailed information about her life to a total stranger," Kevin explained. "Then Mom read more about building a LOK™ and finally accepted Rick's role in facilitating the process." Rosalie finally cooperated with Rick because she understood how daunting the task was for her son, who remembered the paperwork and financial chaos following his father's death.

Rosalie especially enjoyed making the videos with her son. She recounted how she met her husband of sixty-two years, her time as a milliner of stunning hats for women back in more fashionable days, and her memories of Kevin as a young child.

Rosalie passed away after a long battle with diabetes and lymphoma. Kevin grieved while taking care of the final details. He had all the information in mom's LOK™ to lay her to rest and to settle the estate. Thanks to the LOK™ Kevin still had time to devote to his own family, who didn't feel deprived of dad's attention while he was preoccupied with his mother's life, illness, and death.

Support Systems

A LOK Specialist™ can offer support while you get your own or someone else's LOK™ together. The professional clarifies the process of organizing your information and supports you in completing the task effectively.

If you haven't addressed your own estate plan and feel that you don't

have the time or inclination to complete a kit, consider hiring a LOK Specialist™. You supply the information, and the professional will shuffle through all of the materials for your LOK™. (At the same time you can focus on your scrapbook, video, journal, or special instruction letters that you would like to include in the kit.) After a few meetings with the LOK Specialist™ you'll be able to breathe easier, knowing you have established both a LOK™ and a LEAP™ for maximum coverage during an emergency.

Are your LOK™ and LEAP™ designs being kept secret from your loved ones? If you haven't built your LOK™ side by side with your nearest and dearest, now is the time to let them in on your secret weapon. Do they know your ICE Contact? Are they aware of the role you want them to play in your emergency plan? A periodic review of your kit is also essential: As you grow and change so will your LOK™. Keep it current. Lastly, as you review and update the names of the people who execute your contingency plan, consider protecting your intimate blueprint from predators. Your LOK™ contains highly sensitive information about you, so keeping it safe and sound is important too.

Phase

8

Update It

Keep your LOK fresh...

P at yourself on the back. You've just completed the formidable task of getting your kit together. Does your life feel fuller, richer, and more secure? Think about it: Your kit is accurate and up-to-date for the moment, but each year as you change—whether clothing styles, hair color, geographic location, or the people you associate with—your LOK™ is going to change too. In Phase 8, you will learn how to take your LOK™ to the next level so you can keep it current.

Be mindful that as you grow and evolve, so will your LOK™. To live fully, passionately, and confidently each day, reevaluate your LOK™ during the year. Recognize major and minor life events so you can update the kit. You may choose to establish a routine, such as updating information quarterly so your loved ones won't have to deal with outmoded data. Celebrate the year passed, contemplate the adventures ahead, and record those invaluable experiences in the Loved Ones Kit™. Go to www.TheLOK.com. Get the LOK in the Latest System™ and the Checklist of Changes™ to start off a new year.

Life Snapshot

Your LOK™ is a snapshot of your life. We move, change jobs and careers. Our lives morph: Our health, wealth, and communities rapidly transform.

Common examples of life changes your LOK™ captures are: living alone versus with a spouse, moving from an apartment to a house or vice versa, giving birth, developing a medical condition, inheriting money, etc.

When you compiled your LOK™, maybe your snapshot looked like this: You lived with your spouse and children in a large suburban home. A year later, you were in a car accident and suffered back and neck injuries.

You began thrice-weekly visits to specialists who prescribed medicine and healthcare supplements. Not to mention that your career was on hold, and to top this off you moved to a smaller home. Your life snapshot is different from last year, and your LOK™ has to reflect the constant flip-flop of life circumstances.

The kit is built for updates. In an emergency, would your loved ones know the difference between, say, your old health insurance plan at your last company and the name of your new plan from your current employer? What if you changed banks or have new account numbers? Maybe you had a falling out with your estate planning attorney or accountant. Would you want your loved ones to reach out to the wrong person at the wrong time? More importantly, forgetting to record health conditions or allergies could prove deadly. In certain medical situations, not having the right information on hand may mean the difference between life and death.

Scheduled Routines

You may be thinking: How do I stay on top of my LOK™? How do I capture life snapshots when my days are moving ahead on fast-forward? Admittedly, organizing information can be a full-time occupation, since people's lives change so quickly and a plethora of new data is omnipresent.

Schedule time quarterly to update your LOK™. Consistency is key in the routine—the more regular you are, the more your LOK™ will be in sync with your life snapshot. Create a picture that reflects reality.

Starting in the new year, say, select a month and day for reviewing and updating one section at a time in your LOK™. Perhaps you'll choose New Year's Day weekend, a time when you are making new resolutions, putting away holiday decorations, or perhaps watching college football games. You may decide to work on your LOK™ in the middle of January, after the close of the holiday season.

Get out your calendar and select a date. For example, you may choose to do your updates on the fifteenth day of the second month of each quarter. Schedule three months in between dates, i.e., February 15, May 15, August 15, and November 15. During your appointment with your LOK™, reflect on the changes that have taken place within the quarter and note the new information in the kit. Don't be afraid of change. Anticipate activities and events for the following quarter or throughout the year that may alter the information in your kit. If you are working with a LOK Specialist™, schedule appointments with him or her so you can do the revisions together.

To-Do List

Don't get bogged down. Reviewing and updating your LOK™ in just an hour or two every quarter gets your data locked down and keeps it current.

Use the LOK Checklist of Changes™:

☐ *You changed banks.*

☐ *You have new account numbers.*

☐ *You updated your investment portfolio.*

☐ *You added a new asset or cashed one in.*

☐ *You purchased new policies from your insurance agent.*

☐ *You made changes to your estate planning documents.*

☐ You have developed a medical condition.

☐ You are seeing new healthcare practitioners.

☐ You added alternative healthcare, such as acupuncture, chiropractic, Reiki, or massage, to your traditional healthcare regimen.

☐ You moved.

☐ You bought a home.

☐ You got a new dog, cat, or other pet.

☐ You got engaged, married, or divorced.

☐ You are pregnant!

☐ You've changed jobs, been laid off, or left your job to start your own business.

☐ You sold a business, started a new one, or hired a new key employee.

☐ You brought your son or daughter into the family business, or you sold your business to a close family member.

Feel free to add any other life events that have transpired during the quarter.

If you need further help with the LOK Checklist of Changes™, try the following exercise. Place a pen and blank sheets of paper or a notebook in front of you. Fold your hands gently on your lap and sit comfortably. Take a deep breath and close your eyes. Think of the different experiences you have had over the past three months. Reflect on what you know is coming up on the calendar during the next six to twelve months. Open your eyes and write down the events in any order. Then add the events in order to the appropriate sections. Keep adding to the list. Feel free to print out additional checklists at www.TheLOK.com. If you are working with a LOK Specialist™, he or she will walk you through the list quarterly.

At the beginning of each quarterly review, check the list of individuals on your Core Team™. Contact each person to update his or her information. Have any members on your team moved or are there new circumstances that would preclude them from assisting you? Review the information in each section—*Personal* Information, *Medical* Documentation, *Financial* Data, *Legal* Records, and *Community* Activities—and make the appropriate adjustments.

Add new doctors, prescriptions, healthcare treatments, vehicle registration, a renewed passport number, changes to your credit cards, address changes for key contacts, such as your sister who moved from New York City to Los Angeles or a parent who moved from your childhood home to a condominium.

If you changed jobs, note it in your quarterly update. Add your new business card, your boss's and a colleague's name and extension, vehicle registration for the company car, a human resources contact, and information on employer-provided insurance (health, life, and disability) and benefit and retirement plans.

Move through the categories. Update networking and professional group contacts too, and include a copy of your hard copy address book or electronic organizer. Take into account people you spend time with and enjoy. Do you play racquetball with your neighbor? Go on family vacations with two other families during summer break? Perhaps your daughter has a tutor in Spanish, or your son is taking piano lessons. Include everybody! As to *Medical* information: Bear in mind any new doctors and make sure you have all their information up-to-date. Did your primary healthcare practitioner move? Make a note of it in your LOK™. Do you have a newborn at home? Add the baby-sitter and nanny contacts too! What about your *Financial* life? Did you start the year off with a new stockbroker or switch accountants? Have you bought or sold property or other investments? In the *Legal* area, have you changed attorneys or hired a new lawyer? Finally, take a look at the *Community* section of the LOK™. Maybe you have become a member of an exclusive tennis club or your son has joined a little league team. Look at all of the new friends, acquaintances, and business associates in your life; add them to the LOK™ and remove the names of people you no longer interact with. Update, update, update!

In addition, for the first quarterly review, pick a creative activity to celebrate the new year:

- *Create a collage or make a scrapbook. Perhaps you've just taken a winter holiday. Paste your pictures and souvenirs of people and places into a memory book, which can go in your LOK™.*

- *Write, play, and record a song. Have you left an unsupportive relationship, fallen in love with a soul mate, lost a loved one? Write about it. Inform your nearest and dearest of these experiences.*

- *Complete the written eulogy exercise. How do you want loved ones to remember you? Record a video of yourself; include places you've visited, people you've met, the work you've accomplished, and accolades you've received. File any awards you've earned so loved ones can enjoy them too.*

- *Keep a journal. Write down your aspirations: Incorporate photographs, memorabilia, doodles, artwork, jewelry, lyrics, poetry, etc.—all to commemorate you.*

Another fun activity is to reflect on the experiences in your life for which you are grateful. During the holidays, we celebrate our lives together and deepen family bonds. At the Thanksgiving table in my family, each person in turn expresses his joys, sorrows, and gratitude for the past year. Write a poem, prayer, short story, or just a couple of paragraphs about giving thanks or your feelings about a higher power. File it in your LOK™.

For other activities and additional support during quarterly updates, refer to the LOK in the Latest System™ activity book at www.TheLOK.com. The workbook offers activities and advice for updating the kit.

Your Reward

Still dragging your feet? I once heard that: "Procrastination is the art of preparing for yesterday." Don't procrastinate, but do take the time over the years to build and update your LOK™. Go at your own speed: Set aside the requisite time for section-by-section updates. Don't lose sight of the importance of your Core Team™ to make the system work. Set up the team in advance in case anything befalls you while you are assembling

pertinent data. Planning ahead for yourself and loved ones is a gift, and The Loved Ones Kit™ does a job for them that you wouldn't want them to do alone. Keep yourself and others on the most current LOK™ radar screen. When you require assistance and support, your nearest and dearest can plug into the latest information about your life so you get the support you need.

Because you have provided clear instructions for your loved ones to take care of you, your spouse, children, pets, and home, you can rest assured. If you become ill or injured, you can remain confident that your life will be attended to so you can focus your energy and time on recovery. The goal is to offer everyone greater security and peace of mind should tragedy strike. Think of *The Loved Ones Kit* as the path to organizational enlightenment. It introduces a system to organize your money and life for the ones you love.

In the meantime you and your loved ones can watch and celebrate your life—and record those events! Because each LOK™ is a unique blueprint that you create and build upon, it has the power to inform, instruct, and educate. Maybe one day your LOK™ will change your life or the life of a loved one forever.

A s I sit here contemplating the journey you have been on, I applaud your courage and faith to address the most overlooked areas of your life. For the past several years, with loved ones and clients, I have lived through similar catastrophes as those you have just read about. From each experience, I learned there was a way to avoid confusion and exasperation.

I invite you to reflect on experiences in which heartache, frustration, and chaos were the by-products when catastrophe struck. You and your loved ones can now be better prepared when there is upheaval. Celebrate the capacity you and your loved ones have to change and to manage disaster.

Because you and your loved ones are worth protecting, *The Loved Ones Kit* equips you with the ultimate security system. The kit prompts you to take your life to the next level—to be responsible ultimately for yourself and for others. Now explore the universe freely and live fully, passionately, and confidently, knowing that you have secured the future for you and your loved ones.

Introduce the kit to those you love and care for. Share with them the reasons you chose to create a LOK™, and encourage them to do the same. We all have the power to change lives. It begins with an intention, the desire to be good to ourselves and go the extra mile for others. *The Loved Ones Kit* is a labor of love for all who choose to deepen their relationships.

Finally, remember to keep your LOK™ up-to-date and revel in the activities around the quarterly review. Celebrate joy and be confident once you've secured your LOK™, knowing you have everything in the right place at the right time.

The Loved Ones Kit is a gift that I give to you so you can learn to plan ahead. It is a small step for you, and a leap forward for those who love and care about you.

An international expert in business development and strategic planning in top companies, including American Express and Revlon, as well as a Certified Financial Planner™, Jennifer S. Wilkov has over a decade of experience in money relationships. Her company, Evolutionary Strategic Planning (E.S.P.), provides a unique approach to working with clients based on their key needs and desires. As a financial *pioneer*, Jennifer has helped clients design strategies and create multiple income streams so they can swiftly reach their financial goals.

It's no accident that the acronym for her company is E.S.P. Her clients agree: She has a sixth sense! Collaborating with Jennifer means forming a lifelong alliance. Jennifer remains with clients as they evolve, update, and revise their financial plans, making sure that as they grow their wealth grows with them.

Finally, as author and speaker, Jennifer brings her many years of knowledge and wisdom to the table to show you just how easy it is to live fully, passionately, and confidently.

The
Loved Ones
Kit

Recommended
Resources

Newsletter,
Speaking Engagements,
Corporate Programs
and More!

Sign up for The Loved Ones Kit™ newsletter at www.TheLOK.com.

Each month I share insights and information on how to build and keep your LOK™ up-to-date using the enlightened way to organize your finances and life.

Learn more about strategies and creative projects to build your LOK™ and get your Core Team™ ready to leap into action.

I am delighted to be one of the virtual LOK Specialists™ on your team to support your growth and contribute to the greater LOK™ community year after year!

Speaking Engagements

Jennifer S. Wilkov, CFP®, is one of the most sought after female speakers on money relationships and living life to its fullest. Her unique approach to combining emotional intelligence with financial wisdom provides audiences with extraordinary insight, knowledge, and a plan for their money and themselves.

Her enthusiastic presentation of information is transformative, inspiring every area of her audiences' lives.

To have Jennifer S. Wilkov, CFP®, appear at your next event, e-mail speaker@GetMyESP.com or call 1-877-6GET-ESP.

The Loved Ones Kit Website Resources at www.TheLOK.com

The LOK Details Worksheet™

LOK Documents Workbook™

LOK Contact List Workbook™

The Love in a LOK Workbook™

My Core Team & LEAP Worksheet™

LOK Checklist of Changes™

LOK In the Latest System Workbook™

List of Other E.S.P. Websites

www.DatingYourMoney.com

www.GetMyESP.com

General Disclaimer and Limitation of Liability:

The Loved Ones Kit™ is now available as a corporate program for your executive management and key employee team. Take your executive management and employee benefits packages to the next level.

- **Retain key employees: Provide unprecedented assistance to your executive team with a personalized protection plan**

- **Add phenomenal human value to your corporation or company when assisting employees when personal catastrophe strikes**

- **Eliminate confusion about how executive personnel access company benefits**

- **Enhance employee loyalty with a program that cares**

- **Build the trust and security that top executives seek in today's corporate culture**

The Loved Ones Kit Corporate Program™ provides 1 full day of off-site training for your top executives. During the 8-hour program, executive employees focus on the benefit of creating a LOK™ to protect them, loved ones, and their assets.

- **Executives put together a Core Team™ and a Life Emergency Assistance Plan™**

- **Participants identify what is most important in their lives and how to integrate the information in a LOK™**

- **Employees bond through exercises in team building, strategic planning, and building long-lasting customer relationships**

Go to www.TheLOK.com for more information about The Loved Ones Kit Corporate Program™

"Live fully, passionately, and confidently."